Under the Red White and Blue

POSTAL TELEGRAPH – COMMERCIAL CABLES

CLARENCE H. MACKAY, PRESIDENT

CABLEGRAM

RECEIVED AT
555 FIFTH AVE.
AT 46TH STREET,
TEL. VANDERBILT 6395

DELIVERY No.

The Postal Telegraph-Cable Company (Incorporated) transmits and delivers this cablegram subject to the terms and conditions printed on the back of this blank.

20 Dbl.—40462

DESIGN PATENT No. 40529

117 CB 8 18

CAPRI MARCH 19 25

LCD SCRIBNERS FIRMS

      NY (FIFTH AVE AND 48 ST N Y)

CRAZY ABOUT TITLE UNDER THE RED WHITE AND BLUE STOP WHART WOULD DELAY BE.

                             255P   *Fitzgerald*

Under the Red White and Blue

Patriotism, Disenchantment and the
Stubborn Myth of the Great Gatsby

GREIL MARCUS

Yale UNIVERSITY PRESS
NEW HAVEN & LONDON

Frontispiece: Telegram from F. Scott Fitzgerald to his publisher, March 19, 1925.
Archives of Charles Scribner's Sons (C0101); Manuscripts Division,
Special Collections, Princeton University Library.

Published with assistance from the Ronald and Betty Miller Turner Publication Fund.

Published with support from the Fund established in memory of Oliver Baty
Cunningham, a distinguished graduate of the Class of 1917, Yale College, Captain,
15th United States Field Artillery, born in Chicago September 17, 1894, and killed
while on active duty near Thiaucourt, France, September 17, 1918, the twenty-fourth
anniversary of his birth.

Yale University Press books may be purchased in quantity for educational, business, or
promotional use. For information, please e-mail sales.press@yale.edu (U.S. office) or
sales@yaleup.co.uk (U.K. office).

Set in Electra and Nobel types by Tseng Information Systems, Inc.
Printed in the United States of America.

Library of Congress Control Number: 2019948602
ISBN 978-0-300-22890-8 (hardcover : alk. paper)

A catalogue record for this book is available from the British Library.

This paper meets the requirements of ANSI/NISO Z39.48-1992 (Permanence of Paper).

10 9 8 7 6 5 4 3 2 1

For Pearl and Rose, two Minnesota readers

CONTENTS

Under the Red White and Blue

SUBWAY

An interesting story appeared in the *New York Times* a few years ago — a front-page item, April 23, 2013, headlined "Judging 'Gatsby' by Its Cover(s)." Because of the upcoming movie version of *The Great Gatsby* by the Australian director Baz Luhrmann, which was opening two weeks later, there were two new paperback editions of the 1925 F. Scott Fitzgerald novel — the explicit movie tie-in version, with, on the cover, inside a 1920s deco frame, a cutout Leonardo DiCaprio as Jay Gatsby, with Carey Mulligan as Daisy Buchanan below him, the two surrounded by miniatures of Tobey Maguire as Nick Carraway, Elizabeth Debicki as Jordan Baker, Isla Fisher as Myrtle Wilson, and Joel Edgerton as Tom Buchanan, and the un-spoken movie tie-in version, a refurbished edition with the original 1925 spooky-eyes cover art. The story was about which stores, like Walmart, were carrying only the DiCaprio edition, and which were only carrying the other one.

The writer of the story, Julie Bosman, interviewed a book buyer named Kevin Cassem at the revered downtown New York inde-pendent bookstore McNally Jackson. "It's just God-awful," he said about the DiCaprio edition. He went on: "'The Great Gatsby' is a pillar of American literature, and people don't want it messed with. We're selling the classic cover," he said, "and have no intention of selling the new one."

Bosman apparently caught something in Cassem's tone she didn't like. Maybe it was that "people don't want it messed with," or that Cassem, who surely spoke for many, nevertheless felt perfectly fine about speaking for everyone who'd ever read the book, or ever heard of it.

She asked Cassem, in her words, "whether the new, DiCaprio-ed edition of 'Gatsby' would be socially acceptable to carry around in public"—and Cassem took the bait. "I think it would bring shame to anyone who was trying to read that book on the subway," he said. Was he saying that American literature is, so to speak, for people who know how to dress properly, or anyway accessorize? That it's better not to read the book than to read it with the wrong cover?

It was only the age-old language of aesthetic snobbery, which wasn't the language spoken from the screen when the Luhrmann movie played—especially in a place showing it in 3-D.* Movies have always been afraid of the authors whose work they bought up, au-

---

* Or, for that matter, the language spoken on the Pulp! The Classics edition of *The Great Gatsby*, issued that same year, with the Fitzgerald estate on board. "**Wild** parties, **exquisite** cocktails, **fabulous** wealth, **raging** jealousy and **spectacular** deaths," reads the back-cover copy. "Sorry, old sport, but Gatsby has a bigger house than you, prettier friends than you and a Rolls Royce to cart them all around in.

"To a background of popping champagne corks and orchestral jazz, our hero bid to buy out his old adversary, perennial jock, Tom Buchanan and reclaim Daisy, his favourite bit of High Society totty."

Front cover: tough guy in a trench coat, women in evening gowns on either arm. Copy: "*When it came to loving* . . . **He knew which Daisy to pick!**"

thors have always been afraid of what the movies will do to what they sell them, and Luhrmann's was hardly the first effort to transform the book into the medium that Fitzgerald, writing a series of essays called "The Crack-Up" for *Esquire* in 1936, the year before moving to Hollywood to try to find work as a screenwriter after his literary career collapsed, called "a mechanical and communal art that, whether in the hands of Hollywood merchants or Russian idealists, was capable of reflecting only the tritest thought, the most obvious emotion." The trailer for the 1926 silent version, which is all that survives of the film — "No need to *talk* about THIS picture!" read a title card, as if embarrassed in the face of the talkies on the horizon — showed a pack of women in swimsuits charging up a wildly steep, rounding indoor staircase as another horde flooded down, with the director clearly reaching for scale, for scope, to seduce the viewer with opulence, shouting *GIRLS! GIRLS! GIRLS!* like Hungry Joe in *Catch*-22 promising "Multi *dinero*. Multi divorces. Multi ficky-fick all day long."* Gatsby talked as Alan Ladd in 1949 and in 1974 as Robert Redford. They had both been greeted respectfully. But Luhrmann didn't seem afraid of the book. His picture was the first with the ambition to throw Fitzgerald's bitter dismissal of the

---

* Though the picture is lost, one can conjecture. While the leads in 1926 were classy and stolid, there was action in the corners of the story, with Georgia Hale, who the year before entered film history in Chaplin's *The Gold Rush*, as Myrtle Wilson, and William Powell, in 1934 to star in the first of the *Thin Man* movies as the coolest person in America, as the least cool person in *The Great Gatsby*, Myrtle's garage mechanic husband George.

movies back at him, or his ghost, and people responded by throwing Fitzgerald's words back at Luhrmann, which were coded in the argument between movies and literature that began with the birth of the movies and will never end. "The critical fallout is pretty much identical for all my films," said Luhrmann, who had earlier adapted *Romeo and Juliet* and *Moulin Rouge*, when his *Gatsby* came out. "It's not just mild disappointment. It's like I've committed a violent, heinous crime against a personal family member."

Most of the reviews were contemptuous. Underneath you could perhaps hear what you can hear in the debate over which *Great Gatsby* edition to stock: panic over the kidnapping of a delicate, moral flower of American democracy by a foreign sex trafficker. The same note was sounded in Joseph O'Neill's "Pardon Edward Snowden," a short story published in late 2016 in the *New Yorker* that compared the awarding of the Nobel Prize in Literature to Bob Dylan in October to the election of Donald Trump as president of the United States less than a month after that, and ended with a call to protect the good, the true, and the beautiful: "Never give in. Never not resist."

"Luhrmann's vulgarity is designed to win over the young audience, and it suggests that he's less a filmmaker than a music-video director with endless resources and a stunning absence of taste," David Denby said in the *New Yorker*. "Luhrmann's taste is as garish as his hero's, and for much of its running time, his film is an intoxicating cocktail of colour, lights and noise: outlandish party scenes, fantastical New York cityscapes," Tim Walker wrote in the *Independent* in London. "It is crass and superficial—and, yes, it's often difficult to decide whether the director is exposing the hollowness of the era's decadence or simply fetishising the suits." It was a conversation feeding on itself, to the point where critics risked credibility if they deviated too far from the pole. There was talk of "an immortal American tragedy" "buried in Luhrmann's flash and dazzle," "lumbering across the screen like the biggest, trashiest, loudest parade float of all time."

You just can't buy publicity like that. But as Pauline Kael said of *Bonnie and Clyde* in 1967, "it is generally *only* good movies that provoke attacks." Bad movies don't send critics to the ramparts; they file them by genre and move on. Luhrmann had struck a nerve. It might have been that going on a century since Fitzgerald's story first appeared, Luhrmann had completed it: brought it to a fullness that, when the final note was hit, revealed that the movie was what the book had been searching for all along. He tore the tale around the edges, giving it a new frame. He filled in the plot with drunken visions that could make you think a movie director had somehow divined what a long-dead novelist wanted to say but couldn't. "I could have wished the narrator more positively dramatized," Fitzgerald's friend Paul Rosenfeld, a deeply respected music critic, wrote to him in 1925. "Don't you find him, at present, a trifle too passive; and the cause of his narration within himself not sufficiently developed? There were hints, to be sure, but he too was a Great Gatsby." Whether or not he ever read Rosenfeld's letter, Luhrmann picked up those hints and ran them into a story hiding inside the one Fitzgerald told.

The present argues with the past and the past argues with the present, but the present owns the rights. Sometimes, the present can see, or sense, elements of wish, disorder, beauty, and violence that lie latent but unrealized in an artifact of the past, some work that aspired to become a work of art and last forever, and then bring those elements to life and set them loose in the imagination in a way that the putative author never allowed himself or herself to imagine in the first place, or in a way that he or she did imagine, but didn't dare chance. Characters that in the past knew their place may refuse to stick to their assigned roles and try to take over the story. Themes that were once obvious become occluded. Ideas, bits of dialogue, rhythmic shifts that once functioned to advance the plot become both harbingers of tragedy and a reckoning with it.

How that happens with *The Great Gatsby*, a book that for generations has exerted a gravitational pull so insistent that it can seem to have colonized the imagination both of its own country and of people imagining that country from anywhere else, leaving behind an iconographic lingua franca that not only names the lives of people born generations after its author's death but makes them — as with, to almost randomly take a story from the news as I write, the tale of someone who likely would not have even made the papers without the hook that is lodged so deeply in the common imagination:

> A leading K-pop singer has been formally named as a suspect in an investigation into accusations of prostitution and sexual misconduct at nightclubs in South Korea.
>
> The police in Seoul, South Korea, said that the singer, Lee Seung-hyun, 28, who performs under the name Seungri and is a member of the boy band Big Bang, was suspected of "offering sexual services" in 2015.
>
> . . . As Seungri, Lee Seung-hyun has an outsize presence in Seoul's night life and music scene, and also has his

own chain of ramen restaurants. He has cultivated an image evoking F. Scott Fitzgerald's Jay Gatsby, with a solo tour and album under the title "The Great Seungri."

—*New York Times*, March 13, 2019

—is what this book is about. It is about how a certain novel exists on its own terms—as a commercial product, meant to make money and elevate a reputation, and as a story, an exposé and an illumination of the moral life of its characters, the country they inhabit, and the legacy the country's discoverers and founders left for them to reckon with or ignore—and how it also exists in a cultural mirror, where artists other than its author, and readers other than those the author first found, take it up themselves, rewriting it, refashioning it, fulfilling the original in both their own way and its own way. Acknowledging the movie where Gatsby is black and the novels where he is Jewish or female; the tales that follow Daisy Buchanan's daughter or the son Fitzgerald didn't give her into their own dead ends; the detective stories where Gatsbys traveling under different names are unmasked and killed again, or fake their own deaths and return to write new endings; the uncountable student papers following the hundreds of thousands of copies of the book assigned in high school English classes every year;* the movies of 1926, 1949,

---

* To find a frame of reference for an undergraduate course at Berkeley in 2017 called "America Song by Song," professors asked about eighty students, mostly freshmen and sophomores, if they knew who F. Scott Fitzgerald was. Almost everyone did. The same was true for Bob Dylan. FDR was close. Few knew Robert Johnson, more James Dean. Only a handful knew the John Henry song or story, but well over

and 1974; the plays of 1926 and 2006; the TV miniseries and radio dramas; Kate Beaton's 2010 comic strip *Great Gatsbys* ("I hear Gatsby got his money from the Germans," says a flapper at a Gatsby party in a panel titled "The Real Jay Gatsby." "*I* hear he's a Russian count," says a second. "Well," says a third, "I hear he's some kind of harsh metaphor"); Michael Almereyda's *The Great Gatsby (in Five Minutes),** the nearly unwatchable but bizarrely fascinating amateur silent-movie parodies on YouTube (though I've never been able to finish it, I like the seventeen-and-a-half-minute film from 2014, credited to Cornerstone Academy Pictures, Inc., where the big party scene features a few young people in baseball caps dancing languidly in the living room of what appears to be an abandoned house); and Jennifer Love Hewitt as a record company rep in the 1999 film *The Suburbans* trying to pump up the terrified one-hit-wonder eighties band of the same name now on tour for the first time in fifteen years with "So! We beat on, boats against the current, borne ceaselessly into the past!" which doesn't make them feel any better, it seems to me that this gleefully unending conversation is conjured most ambitiously, most deliriously, and most witheringly in Baz Luhrmann's movie and in the 2006 six-and-a-half-

---

two-thirds knew Tupac Shakur and more knew Amy Winehouse. More people than not had seen *The Godfather.* Almost no one had heard of Ayn Rand.

* "'The Silverlake Gatsby,'" Almereyda said in 2018 of the Los Angeles neighborhood where the film was shot. "An extremely low-budget enterprise made while Baz Luhrmann was spending millions on his version. (Our main expense was tacos.)" It screened at the New York Film Festival in 2011 and then vanished.

hour word-for-word theatrical reading of *Gatz*—maybe because it took that long, into the twenty-first century, for the book to rewrite itself, guiding other hands as they flattered themselves into thinking they were acting on their own. Those works distort the original without diminishing it, do damage to it without leaving scars, translate it into other forms of English, leaving behind a richer work now more open to new readers, and new times, than it was before, and simply to follow how that happens is a story in and of itself. It is the story of a great common art project, where culture is a matter of erasing questions of what should matter and what actually does matter: as Annie Ernaux wrote in 1992 in *Simple Passion* of the "cultural standards governing emotion which have influenced me since childhood," "*Gone With the Wind, Phèdre* or the songs of Edith Piaf are just as decisive as the Oedipus complex." And at its heart—reaching backward and forward in time so that it captures stories as far apart as those in *Moby-Dick* and *Mad Men*; reappearing all but whole in Raymond Chandler's *The Long Goodbye* and Philip Roth's *The Human Stain*; echoing through cultural productions as disparate as an Andy Kaufman stand-up routine and a half-dozen Ross Macdonald mysteries—it is a patriotic project: taking a novel as part of a patrimony. "My two American sons had a pretty good education (I like to hope)," wrote the British-born film historian David Thomson in 2018, "but I'm not sure the Founding Fathers meant that much to them. Washington is a dollar bill, Hamilton is that guy in a musical. But aren't their real founding fathers Gatsby, Charles Foster Kane, and Holden Caulfield?"

A PATRIOTIC SWERVE

Rick, you're not only a sentimentalist, but you've become a patriot!
— *Claude Rains to Humphrey Bogart, Casablanca, 1942*

CRAZY ABOUT THE TITLE UNDER THE RED WHITE AND BLUE STOP
WHART WOULD DELAY BE
— *telegram from F. Scott Fitzgerald to his publisher, March 19, 1925*

In America, the humblest harmony is still an incredible dream.
— *Edmund Wilson, "Night Thoughts in Paris: A Rhapsody," New Republic, March 15, 1922*

Once upon a time, there was something that called itself the People's Bicentennial Commission. Launched in 1974 by the then leftist publicist Jeremy Rifkin, in later years a trend theorist and adviser to both the European Union and the People's Republic of China, the group, which claimed a network of books, magazines, buttons, bumper stickers, radio programs, television documentaries, newspaper columns, and lesson plans for elementary and high schools, promised to offer a real, people's, revolutionary-at-its-heart America, as opposed to the official America promulgated for bicentennial purposes by various hucksters and government agencies. (Watergate tapes researchers would later find President Richard Nixon, shortly after his reelection in 1972, discussing the need for a "house Jew" to "handle the Bicentennial and all that nonsense.") PBC members were self-described New Patriots; you could become a New Patriot by joining the PBC.

According to the PBC, Americans were to be divided into Patriots and Tories—in fact, all American history, and the American present, could and should be seen this way. Patriots were those the PBC aligned on the side of social and economic justice, defined in a manner conventionally rendered as progressive; Tories were all those perceived by the PBC to have resisted such values. Thus Alexander Hamilton, despite his role in the revolution, not to mention the founding of the republic, was really a Tory, as were, in the group's blacklist, corporation executives, bankers, factory foremen, and unsympathetic high school principals. And presumably the notorious racist James O. Eastland, Democrat of Mississippi, in 1976 chairman of the Senate Judiciary Committee, which that year issued a report on the PBC titled "The Attempt to Steal the Bicentennial."

There was nothing troublesome about PBC patriotism; all it took was a correct stand on the correct issues, and maybe a membership card. The PBC program was equally simple. Patriots should expose Tories. Political candidates should be forced to sign loyalty oaths to the creed of the revolution. PBC political clubs should ask to have copies of the Declaration of Independence posted outside polling places, "so that citizens may spend their time thinking about self-evident truths." There's nothing to suggest that patriotism is a burden: the burden of loving one's sometimes hateful country.

I wonder if the sixth episode of the sixth season of *The Sopranos*, which aired on April 16, 2006, would have fit the PBC charge. Vito

Spatafore—the most reliable and loyal captain in the New Jersey crime family headed by Tony Soprano—is on the run. Vito has a wife, two kids, the requisite mistress, but he's been seen in a gay bar dressed like the biker in the Village People. The mob wants him dead; he's dishonored them all.

Heading north, Vito's been driving for hours. His cell phone rings; he throws it out the window. He has no idea where he is. His car breaks down. He makes it into the next town, finds an inn, puts his gun under his pillow.

The next day he wakes up in another country: in a New Hampshire village where gay people walk the streets without fear. In a diner, looks pass between Vito and the counterman. A male couple comes in, sits down, and begins speaking in a language Vito has only heard in the dark, never in the light of day. He's confused: what does it mean to be in a place where, for the first time in your life, you might feel at home in your own skin? Could that even be right?

He goes into an antique shop. He picks up a vase, and the gay owner compliments him on his taste: "That's the most expensive item in the store." But then Vito sees something else, probably the cheapest item in the store: an old New Hampshire license plate: LIVE FREE OR DIE reads the motto across the top.

The phrase burns into Vito's mind. You can see his face change. The phrase was coined in 1809 by General John Stark, a New Hampshire hero of the Revolutionary War, on the occasion of the thirty-second reunion of veterans of the 1777 Battle of Bennington, Vermont: too ill to attend, Stark sent a toast. "Live free or die," another man read for him. "Death is not the worst of evils." The words echoed across the new nation, down through the decades; in 1945, with the end of the Second World War, New Hampshire took the first four words and put them on every road in the state.

Vito stares. LIVE FREE OR DIE — it's as if the metal can talk. It's just a license plate; for him it might as well be the Declaration of Independence, ringing its bell. "We hold these truths to be self-evident, that all men are created equal, that they are endowed by their Creator with certain unalienable Rights, that among these are Life, Liberty, and the pursuit of Happiness," Jefferson wrote — and suddenly, as it has for so many for so long, through that license plate the Declaration is speaking to Vito as if it were addressed directly to him. *Live free or die* — what if all this, the shock in his face says, was meant for him as much as anyone?

It's one of those signal moments when the whole weight of the national story, its promises and betrayals, hits home — leaving the citizen at once part of a community and completely alone. It doesn't matter that on July 4, 1776, when the Declaration of Independence was presented, everyone understood that all men meant men, not women; whites, not blacks; Christians, not Jews or Hindus or Parsees; decent people, not Sodomites. The idea that "all men are created equal" was not a "self-evident truth," John Pettit of Indiana said on the floor of the Senate in 1853; it was "a self-evident lie." It was in the midst of the debates over the Kansas-Nebraska Act; Pettit was arguing for the voiding of the Missouri Compromise of 1820 and opening the territories to slavery. He didn't go unanswered: "The great declaration cost our forefathers too dear," Senator Benjamin Franklin Wade of Ohio replied to Pettit, "to be so lightly thrown away by their children."

Abraham Lincoln read these debates from his oblivion in

Springfield, Illinois; he was a forty-four-year-old lawyer who had served one term in Congress before being turned out of office. Pettit's words and the words against him brought Lincoln back to the world. Soon he was speaking as if the Declaration of Independence contained all the words the nation ever needed to hear—and in a certain sense, it didn't matter that Lincoln did not believe that once men and women left the hand of their creator, they were equal on earth. Pettit called "the Declaration of Independence a 'self-evident' lie," Lincoln said in Peoria in 1854, answering a speech by Stephen Douglas. "If it had been said in old Independence Hall seventy-eight years ago, the very doorkeeper would have throttled the man, and thrust him into the street." That might have been a fairy tale; the Declaration of Independence itself might be a fairy tale, but not one that can be given an ending, happy or not. The affirmation in the Declaration was boundless; no limits placed on it hold.

"Life, liberty, and the pursuit of happiness"—it's what the rest of the world understands by America when America isn't forcing the rest of the world to understand America as something else. "We are caught in a world of limits where there's no such thing as the self-made man," said a graduate student in France just a week before Vito arrived in New Hampshire; Claire de la Vigne was speaking to a *New York Times* reporter about the French university system, where doors were meant to be closed, not opened. "We are never taught the idea of the American dream, where everything is possible," she said. It's what Americans understand by America, when the base facts of everyday American life somehow recede, and an idea of America takes their place.

In *The Enthusiast*, a novel from 2009 by the one-time screen-writer Charlie Haas, a scientist is in a care facility trying to recover from brain damage. His father is trying to reintroduce him to time, place, names, faces.

> Dad and Barney sat at the desk with the datebook in front of them. "Okay," Dad said, "what's something you might have to do this afternoon?"
>
> "Go to a meeting," Barney said.
>
> "Okay. So you write that in there."
>
> Barney scrawled *meeting* in the 3:00 P.M. slot. "We're going to have a country," he said. "We have some farmers coming, and some horseshoe guys."
>
> "Blacksmiths?" Dad said.
>
> "Yes," Barney said. "So we get liberty. And we wear wigs in the room."

This doesn't even have the weight of a fairy tale, or of a dream you can just barely remember—and yet it's inescapable, and unbreak-able.

There's a way in which you can see every American story as a version of the Declaration of Independence: every story an at-tempt to make it true, or prove it a lie. In 1941, Henry Luce called the twentieth century "The American Century": he meant that was the century when America became a colossus from which the rest of the world would have to step back, trembling with awe. But if that American century was truly American, you can almost hear Lincoln reminding us—or, if not Lincoln, the doorkeeper at Inde-pendence Hall—then the story of the American century is the story of all sorts of previously excluded, marginalized, scorned, despised, ignored, or enslaved people—laborers, women, African-Americans, Asian-Americans, Jews, Latinos, gay men and women—entering into full citizenship and a full participation in national life. If not full citizenship, a more complete citizenship than even Lincoln or the doorkeeper could have imagined—as, again and again, decade after decade, those words from the Declaration of Independence sounded as if for the first time.

Another scene from 2006, around the time Vito Spatafore made his escape: a meeting in Cambridge, Massachusetts, and not that far, for its goals, from Barney and his father trying to bring the meeting in Independence Hall into focus. A group of sixteen people—historians, critics, poets, novelists, professors—sat around a table trying to determine what would and what would not be included in a thousand-page, two-hundred-chapter "New Literary History of America." *"All God's Dangers—The Life of Nate Shaw,"* one person said. No one responded. Few people had heard of the book; only two had read it.

The book appeared in 1975, under the imprint of the most prestigious publisher in the country, and then it disappeared. Why? It won a National Book Award; reviews were like trumpets. But somehow the tale told by Nate Shaw—the name the historian Theodore Rosengarten gave to one Ned Cobb, whose name had to be changed, in 1975, to protect his family from white violence, who was born in Alabama in 1885 and died there in 1973, and who, late in his life, over hundreds of hours, spun Rosengarten the story of his life—did not fit the American story as it was, then, being reconstructed once again. This was a man whose father had been a slave, and who, as if he were, as in the song he would have grown up hearing, his own John Henry, reveled in his superiority over others be they black and white — in mind, body, will, desire, courage, and wit, as a worker, a capitalist with his own mules, truck, and automobile, free and clear, a man of his word. "All men are created equal" — but what men and women become is not equal, and proving himself in that arena was America to Ned Cobb. "I was climbin up in the world just like a boy climbin a tree. And I fell just as easy, too." It's 1931, in the heart of the Depression, and a banker is squeezing him.

> "Bring me the cotton this fall, bring me the cotton." When
> he told me that I got disheartened. I didn't want him messin
> with me — still, I didn't let him take a mortgage on anything
> I owned. I was my own man, had been for many years, and
> God knows I weren't goin to turn the calendar back on myself.

You can hear it in the cadence, in the choice of words, a man speaking his own language: "I weren't goin to turn the calendar back on myself." This is someone for whom liberty was real — as real in its absence as when he can hold it in his hands. At twenty-one, in 1906, he set out to raise his first cotton crop; in 1932 he stood for the Alabama Sharecroppers Union against a gang of sheriffs sent to seize a friend's property, and paid for his stand with twelve years in prison. He found God. He walked out of prison. He lived a new life.

From his first day on his own, he was by fact and determination not someone who could be reduced to a type, a symbol, or made to stand for someone else's cause. Against all odds he had achieved what the country promised him: "life," on his own ground; "liberty," reached for, grasped, acted out, taken from him; "the pursuit of happiness"—which for him meant the satisfaction of work and, at the end of his life, firing his revolver in the air. "I shoots it sometimes just to see if it will yet answer me," he said. "I throw it to the air and ask for all six shots: YAW YAW YAW YAW YAW YAW." The story came off the pages with suspense, order, clarity, and drama, as if Shaw had long before determined not to quit the country without leaving a piece of his own behind.

His own—all he had, to pass on to whoever might stumble upon the now-forgotten book made of his particular pursuit of happiness. But if the people gathered to choose the books of the American story had not heard of Nate Shaw, in a certain way, Vito, standing in that New Hampshire antique store, was hearing Nate Shaw speak as he read the words on the license plate.

On *The Sopranos*, as Vito read LIVE FREE OR DIE, a song began to come up on the soundtrack: "4th of July," written by Dave Alvin, recorded in 1987 by the Los Angeles punk band X. It's thrilling, and it's heartbreaking; a couple's marriage is breaking up, but it's the Fourth of July. The feeling in the song is that by failing their marriage they are failing the country: "We gave up trying so long ago." The stirring reach in the way the man and woman sing the melody, a reach that falls so far short of its grasp, tells you they aren't speaking only for themselves. A shared idea is dying within them.

Jefferson gave Gatsby the right to his mission; did Gatsby fail Jefferson? The two people in "4th of July"—can Jefferson save their marriage? Can they save the country? Vito Spatafore, Ned Cobb, Jay Gatsby, the L.A. couple as John Doe and Exene Cervenka sing their song—they are all patriots, trying to define their country as if their choices are their own.

Most Americans, as the late political theorist John H. Schaar wrote in 1973, may be "simply without patriotism. . . . They do not think unpatriotic thoughts, but they do not think patriotic thoughts either." That can make the appearance of patriotism—the way it throws both particular Americans and America as such, either as fact, history, or idea, into relief—a shock. I remember that: at the time, with its newspaper ads and mailings, its call for 250,000 people to mass in Washington, D.C., on July 4, 1976, its promise of a $25,000 award to any secretary whose testimony of mistreatment led to the successful prosecution of her employer, the People's Bicentennial Commission and its loyalty oaths made me think of three southern, conservative members of the House Judiciary Committee, Democrats James Mann of South Carolina and Walter Flowers of Alabama, and Republican Caldwell Butler of Virginia, who in 1974 voted to advance a bill of impeachment against Richard Nixon. In PBC terms they were obvious Tories; in a PBC America it would have been irrelevant that, as public representatives, they made distinct efforts to trace a line between their particular responsibilities and the founding of the country, to understand who they were and how they fit into the moral map of the republic.

Three speakers:

One ever feels his two-ness—an American, a Negro; two souls, two thoughts, two unreconciled strivings; two warring ideals in one dark body.
—W. E. B. Du Bois, "Strivings of the Negro People," *Atlantic*, 1897

The patriot is one who is grateful for a legacy and recognizes that the legacy makes him a debtor. There is a whole way of being in the world, captured best by the word reverence, which defines life by its debts: one is what one owes, what one acknowledges as a rightful debt or obligation. The patriot moves within that mentality. The gift of land, people, language, gods, memories, and customs, which is the patrimony of the patriot, defines who he or she is. Patrimony is mixed with person; the two are barely separable. The very tone and rhythm of a life, the shapes of perception, the textures of its hopes and fears come from membership in a territorially rooted group. The conscious patriot is one who feels deeply indebted for these gifts, grateful to the people and places through which they came, and determined to defend the legacy against enemies and pass it unspoiled to those who will come after.

But such primary experiences are nearly inaccessible to us. We are taught to define our lives not by our debts and legacies, but by our rights and opportunities.

—John H. Schaar, "The Case for Patriotism," *American Review* 17, May 1973

When I think of Greenwich Village, it is almost with tears. For there this battered battalion dress their guns against a whole nation . . . from the darkest corners of the country they have fled for comfort and asylum. You may think them feeble and ridiculous—but feebleness is always relative. It may require as much force of character and as much independent thought for one of these to leave his Kansas home and espouse the opinions of Freud as for Wagner to achieve new harmonies or Einstein to conceive a finite universe. The thought of them makes me respond with a sharp gust of sympathy, precisely because they *are* ridiculous and yet stand for something noble. And one is touched by something like reverence when one finds among this strange indifferent people, to whom the rest of the world is a newspaper story, history a tedious legend and abstract thought a form of insanity, a man who really knows on what stage he is playing, for what drama he has been cast. By his realization he makes us realize, too, for what drama our setting is the setting: for the drama of humanity, in a sense, no setting can be trivial or mean. Gopher Prairie itself, in all its ludicrousness and futility when the human spirit rears itself there, has its importance and its dignity.

And now that a breach has been made what a flood might sweep off the dam!—what a thundering torrent of energy, of enthusiasm, of life! Things are always beginning in America; we are always on the verge of great adventures. History seems to lie before us instead of behind.

—Edmund Wilson, "Night Thoughts in Paris"

To actually read these passages is to pay as close attention to the voice of each writer as to his words. Du Bois, meditating on truths that predate his time and which he doesn't seem to expect to change, is stymied, perplexed, quietly angry, yet so full of a sort of determination it perhaps suggests the bridging of gaps he is saying cannot be bridged. Schaar, with his eyes on the past—not merely the American past, but the past as such, the past as something constantly surrounding the present—speaks in tones of regret. His cadences are measured and restrained, and what is measured is the pain of loss, the loss of the way of being in the world he is describing. All this is evident well before his final disclaimer: that we are not taught the rich and complex values of patriotism, of a sense of membership in a patrimony, but, by his judgment, the comparatively impoverished values that imply, legitimate, and drive the separation of each citizen from every other as the positive basis of American society.

Both Schaar and Du Bois speak as realists. Their words communicate a refusal to grant a single assurance they don't see as justified by the disappointments and betrayals of the American story.

But Wilson's "In America, the humblest harmony is still an incredible dream"—and harmony not as consensus, or lack of fundamental disagreements, but an essential harmony, a recognition of uniquely American things shared, which may be values, or historical events, or nothing more than a few made-up stories—is at the heart of what both Du Bois and Schaar are saying. They're saying that whatever the American reality, or even the American fate, the possibilities of such a harmony can't be decently abandoned; that harmony is a necessity if Americans are to even come close to keeping the promises on which America was founded. Those were the promises that flowed instantly from the original justification of America as something new under the sun, that place of life, liberty, and the pursuit of happiness—with the last idea so explosive that in Paris, in 1794, facing the Convention in Year Two of the Revolution, eighteen years after the publication of the Declaration of Independence, Antoine Saint-Just, of the Committee of Public Safety, still picking up Jefferson's echo, could say the word in wonder: "Happiness is a new idea in Europe." It was even the promise as it was reclaimed on March 4, 1865, with the Civil War not yet over, in Lincoln's Second Inaugural Address—when, with the prophecy that the war might rightly continue "until all the wealth piled by the bond-man's two hundred and fifty years of unrequited toil shall be sunk, and until every drop of blood drawn with the lash, shall be paid by another drawn with the sword," he incorporated the truth that the betrayal of those promises preceded the promises themselves into the landscape of official American thought, where, as the story Lincoln was telling has continued to play out, it has been officially buried ever since.

To turn from the gloom of Du Bois and Schaar to the late-night meditations of a twenty-six-year-old Edmund Wilson, thinking of America from a distance, is that patriotic shock. It might be necessary to read what he wrote slowly to appreciate how bizarre it is.

When I first came to Berkeley, as a freshman in 1963, a campus veteran told me—parroting Czesław Miłosz in *The Captive Mind*, I found out later—that Berkeley and Greenwich Village were the only places in America where a person could be truly free. Wilson begins with this cozily embattled fallacy: a farther shore from the kind of patriotism lined out by Schaar, who at the time taught political theory at Berkeley, can hardly be imagined. And yet—or, perhaps, and so—Wilson drives straight back into what he called the darkest corners of the country and embraces them with all the restraint of a Fourth of July orator. Suddenly he has delivered himself from the repression of the American present, precisely the present in which Fitzgerald set *The Great Gatsby*—1922, to Fitzgerald the Jazz Age at its apogee—as if only the future were of any consequence. But there is that hint of condescension in Wilson's "Gopher Prairie itself"—which is matched by Wilson's naming as one of his dark corners a fictional place, the Minnesota town in Sinclair Lewis's 1920 novel *Main Street*, rather than a real place like such Gopher Prairie models as St. Cloud or Little Falls, which in 1922 Wilson might not have heard of. And that is itself a match for the way that, perhaps in doubts that not even the most visionary moment can banish, Wilson then abandons the pull of American specifics for a manifesto of American mysticism. It's as if he's speaking, against the odds he has been careful to establish in advance, to fix those things Americans can recognize—those attributes by which they recognize each other—the feeling that "things are always beginning in America," blown up in an instant with exclamation points into images of a great dam breaking and a flood of— not ideas, not justice, not even freedom (which is what Wilson had started with in that invocation of the rebels of Greenwich Village, but which is somehow no longer the question), but "of energy, of enthusiasm, of life!" And this is because what Wilson was working out in Paris was a leap of faith—a leap straight across what were to Lincoln almost predestined American crimes and divisions, the crimes and divisions that were the source of Du Bois's torment.

The desperation in Wilson's voice is as palpable as the joy. A moment later in "Night Thoughts" he will pull back again: America has become a monster of banality, unfit for a thinking man. But he can't quit with this. He returns as an American St. George come not to slay the dragon but magically transform it. "Our enemy"—the dragon America—"offers huger bulk than the enemy in Europe"—Europe as a society, a civilization, precisely what was overthrown and stripped of its legitimacy in the first sentence of the Declaration of Independence—"but he is much less firmly rooted. Two generations might rout him. To arms then! Let me return; I shall not cease from mental fight nor shall my sword rest in my hand till intolerance has been stricken from the laws, till the time-clock has been beaten to a punch-bowl!"

In the great tradition of John Wesley Harding, who never made a foolish move, Wilson doesn't choose a foolish word. The struggle he is tracing is a matter of spiritual life or death for him, and—in the sense that a true patriot, one who truly accepts the gift of a patrimony, does not merely affirm but embodies the republic—for the country too. Thus Wilson's language is overblown, with every pretension undercut by parody (the lines from Blake on "mental fight" and "my sword" sounding as absurd here as they are painful and stirring in "Jerusalem," or the Nietzschean "till intolerance has been stricken from the laws" taken down a peg by "till the time-clock has been beaten to a punch bowl").

This ballooning way of speaking is the language, or a language, of American patriotism, and its affirmation a settling of affairs. It sweeps right by Du Bois's own affirmation of what cannot be resolved, even though Wilson's words do not quite leave Du Bois's statement of the facts out. "How far can love for my oppressed race accord with love for the oppressing country?" Du Bois wrote in 1961, two years before his death at ninety-five, in exile in Ghana. "And when these loyalties diverge, where shall my soul find refuge?"* Du Bois speaks as a black American, and the question he insists on contains all Americans who have been systematically refused America's promises and excluded from its patrimony—or who know in their bones that, their achievements and reputations and riches to the contrary, they might be. "Jews want to be American so bad," the singer Randy Newman said in 1994. "Dylan ran away from it as far as he could. Irving Berlin wrote Alabamy. I know I'm American, but I feel—they could *turn* on me at any moment."†

Schaar writes of America, an invented political and moral society, as a place where patriotism is not simply a matter of in-

---

* Du Bois had traveled to Ghana to work on an encyclopedia of African culture and its presence around the world; he remained after the U.S. government, targeting him as a subversive and a Communist, refused to renew his passport. His death date was August 27, 1963, one day before the March on Washington for Jobs and Freedom, where his name was sent out over the crowd.

† In a version of his song "Dixie Flyer," originally from his 1988 album *Land of Dreams* but redone as a solo piano piece in 2011 on *The Randy Newman Songbook Vol. 2*, Newman said the same thing, but with a rage that wasn't there before. The number opens with a lovely slow pace, which intensifies just slightly as it turns toward ragtime, and then with no shift you can quite fix, Newman's lilt deepens into a warm heartbreak, and his account of traveling from Los Angeles during the war to his mother's hometown of New Orleans, meeting his new relatives, almost breaks the song: "Trying to do like the gentiles do / Christ, they wanted to be gentiles too / Who wouldn't down there, wouldn't you? An American Christian / God damn!"

heritance or the lack of it: in his America, patriotism is an earned choice, an earned recognition. Wilson, fifty-one years earlier, agreed when he spoke as baldly as he dared about a mental fight, a battle he would carry on, as a critic and a reporter, to rout the enemy, to make the fairy tale of American harmony he glimpsed one night in Paris come true.

When one speaks of patriotism in America one must recognize an inevitable division of self in the very act of speaking—and in that sense Du Bois's statement can serve for anyone. America is big, conformist, monolithic, faceless, and cruel, and its economic game is fixed. To achieve any sense of freedom the first impulse is to separate oneself, either by following the trail of countless American Ishmaels, or by accepting one's own homogeneous familiars: of family, background, region, race, religion. Yet America is too big, complex, and too various for any single mind to take in—and in the realization of an enormous place finally justified and held together by little more than a few phrases from old documents comes the yearning to make America whole by seeing it clearly: by pursuing that patrimony, discovering it as students and immigrants do, retrieving it as historians do, inventing it as novelists do, or by simply affirming it, as, even if thinking neither patriotic or unpatriotic thoughts, anyone does when he or she votes. That may have been how Fitzgerald understood the story he was telling when less than a month before his publication date he asked if he could change "The Great Gatsby" to "Under the Red White and Blue." What is it that Americans share? In what images of crime or beauty do Americans uniquely recognize themselves as no others would, recognize that in an essential way they are linked, that they can carry on certain conversations about certain things—about, say, whether in 2017 a white artist had the right to paint her own version of the body of Emmett Till, as it had been put out for public view in 1955, bloated and unrecognizable, as it was found after it was thrown into the Tallahatchie River in Mississippi, where the fourteen-year-old from Chicago was lynched for speaking to a white woman, because the story of Emmett Till is as much a part of the American grain as the story of John Wilkes Booth or the story of Harriet Tubman—that others would not or could not think to take up at all? What if Fitzgerald's goal was to create just such a thing, a doubled, shifting image of beauty and crime?

You probably can't raise such questions without realizing there may be no good answers. But you can't wear out such questions either. Schaar's words, like Wilson's, point toward a way of being not merely in the world but in America: suspicious, wary, looking over your shoulder, and yet accepting of something like a common fate.

The idea of the patriot as one who embodies the republic doesn't point toward the pretentious or the grand. A civil rights worker in Mississippi in 1964, linking people to the Declaration of Independence by trying to persuade them to attempt to vote, is embodying the republic. Lady Gaga, speaking on television to Stephen Colbert on October 5, 2018, the night before Brett Kavanaugh was confirmed in the Senate as a justice of the Supreme Court by a vote of 50–48, after being accused by Christine Blasey Ford of sexually assaulting her when she was a teenager, describing the process of repression, denial, and self-protection that follows sexual assault—"The brain changes. . . . It takes the trauma, and it puts it in a box, and it files it away and shuts it, so that we can survive"—and how she understood the drama that at that moment was convulsing the nation, speaking with deadly seriousness in an almost pedagogical mode, pointing her finger, jabbing it into the air, saying, "But what I believe I have seen, is that when this woman saw, that Judge Kavanaugh was going to be possibly put, in the *highest position* of power in the judicial system of this country, she was triggered. And that box opened. And when that box opened, she was brave enough, to share it with the world: to protect this country"—she was, by the sense of love and jeopardy she put into her last four words, embodying the republic. Many of those on the House Judiciary Committee, forty-four years before, by what they said and the manner in which they said it, embodied the republic, for a time, and none so powerfully as Barbara Jordan of Texas, when three days before the committee would vote she read American history through herself: "Earlier today, we heard the beginning of the Preamble to the Constitution of the United States: 'We, the people.' It's a very eloquent beginning. But when that document was completed on the seventeenth of September 1787, I was not included in 'We, the people.' I felt somehow for many years that George Washington and Alexander Hamilton just left me out by mistake. But through the process of amendment, interpretation, and court decision, I have finally been included in 'We, the people.'" "Today I am an inquisitor," she said, and to rescue the word from its common context returned it to Hamilton himself, writing in number sixty-five of *The Federalist*, "Who can so properly be the inquisitors for the nation as the representatives of the nation themselves?" saying, as she did so, that as once Hamilton embodied the republic, she did now. Those who honestly and visibly refuse to let the republic stop short of itself embody it.

Visibly is the key word: publicly. Edmund Wilson spoke almost mysteriously of "a man who really knows on what stage he is playing, for what drama he has been cast. By his realization he makes us realize, too, for what drama our setting is the setting." To say that this can mean anything is to point to the force of what Wilson said, not its weakness—a force for which Wilson found a vessel only thirty-three years after he first tried to describe it. "It was as if he had not only foreseen the drama but had even seen all around it," Wilson wrote in 1953, on Lincoln and "The Union as Religious Mysticism," "with a kind of poetic objectivity, aware of the various points of view that the world must take toward its protagonist. In the poem that Lincoln lived, Booth had been prepared for, too, and the tragic conclusion was necessary to justify all the rest. It was dramatically and morally inevitable that this prophet who had overruled opposition and sent thousands of men to their deaths should finally attest his good faith by laying down his own life with theirs." The American patriot is the person who, embodying the debts and possibilities of American life, dramatizes them in view of others. That is both an instinct—the yearning for and affirmation of harmony—and a role—the acting out of harmony.

The notion of a whole way of being in the world is both the treasure of patriotism and the key to it. It is a constant, renewing asking of the questions that make up a kind of patriot chorus, that *What is it that Americans share?* the phrase asking over and over what is essential and unique in their history, their experience, and their fate.

In Paris, in 1922, Wilson began what he called his rhapsody thinking of Futurism, "born in Italy, where the weight of the past lies heaviest." "But *I* can scarcely adore the locomotive," he wrote. "I know it all too well." He went on to wonder at his dreams for America, to criticize America as brutally as he could manage, to pull away, back and forth, back and forth, the double vision of the American patriot at work, searching for at least a night's truce with itself. He turned back finally to the image of the rails, and all the stops came out. The American train was America itself, as if at any given moment it was every American in turn, from those of the founding generations long past Wilson's own, each with his or her own mind, will, and memory. He could have been singing Bruce Springsteen's revision of the old gospel blues "This Train," with its "This train, don't carry no gamblers," into his patriotic anthem "Land of Hope and Dreams," where the American train carried "whores and gamblers," "losers and winners," and "fools and kings":

> Where there is a petulance and a sadness in the piping of
> the French engines, I shall hear in the American ones an
> eagerness and a zest: they have elbow room here for their
> racing; they can drive on as far as they like; they have an un-
> known country to explore, a country that no one has ever
> heard of. — What sort of men are these who live in name-
> less towns? At a distance, they seem neither intelligent nor
> colorful nor fine — scarcely members of the same race as the
> beings who have built civilization. But I know that in the wide
> spaces of that wilderness, in the life of that loose abundant
> world, for all the reign of mediocrity and the tyranny of intol-

erance, there is a new freshness and freedom to be brought to the function of mankind — the function which, in the long run, we shall never be able to get out of: staring out in wonder and dismay at the mysterious shapes of the world, either to ask ourselves what laws move them or, combining those shapes anew, to make shift to create a nobler world in which our souls may find a home.

That "we shall never be able to get out of": with his last-minute attempt to fly the flag through the title of his book, and setting his story in the year in which Wilson published his manifesto, this is the path that Fitzgerald set out to follow, to see where it led, if it led anywhere at all.

A BOOK EVERYONE HAS HEARD OF

There are minds that have gone as far as Shakespeare into the universe. And hardly a mortal man, who, at some time or other, has not felt as great thoughts in him as any you will find in Hamlet. We must not inferentially malign mankind for the sake of any one man, whoever he may be. This is too cheap a purchase of contentment for conscious mediocrity to make. Besides, this absolute and unconditional adoration of Shakespeare has grown to be part of our Anglo Saxon superstitions. . . . You must believe in Shakespeare's unapproachability, or quit the country. But what sort of belief is this for an American, a man who is bound to carry republican progressiveness into Literature, as well as into Life? Believe me, my friends, that Shakespeares are this day being born on the banks of the Ohio.

—Herman Melville, "Hawthorne and His Mosses," New York Literary World, *August 24, 1850*

I think my novel is about the best American novel ever written.

—F. Scott Fitzgerald to Maxwell Perkins, c. *August 25, 1924*

One of the most interesting things about *The Great Gatsby*, either as a book within its own covers or for all that in the near-century since it first appeared it has drawn into itself and sent back into the world—that whole panoply of echoes from Raymond Chandler's Terry Lennox in *The Long Goodbye* in 1953 to Ross Macdonald's John Brown in *The Galton Case* in 1959 and his Nick Carraway of a detective, Lew Archer, as "a ghost in the sense of just being a tone of voice," to Philip Roth's Coleman Silk in *The Human Stain* in 2000 and Matthew Weiner and Jon Hamm's Don Draper in *Mad Men* from 2007 to 2015, the chain of American avatars from Sojourner Truth to Cary Grant to Barack Obama—is that it can make all questions of sanctity and violation, literature and trash, the vulgar and the truth, absolutely moot.

The story has made its place in the common imagination. It remains there whole and in pieces, as a bare map of a source that has disappeared into a kind of emotional folklore, a socially inherited but seemingly individual response. "*Gatsby* is certainly the most important book in my life," Macdonald said in 1972, in an interview with the critic Paul Nelson, then pushing past himself with "I think this is true for all Americans." Either he was identifying himself with the entire story of the republic, as Americans tend to do, or he was insisting that *The Great Gatsby* in and of itself told the story of all Americans, whether they had ever read it or not, whether or not what Macdonald or for that matter Fitzgerald had to say made any sense to them at all. Any number of Americans might claim *Gone with the Wind* or *Fahrenheit 451* or *Invisible Man* or *The Shining*, but what do they know? The book itself is a test of citizenship, Macdonald seemed to be saying. He seemed to be saying that if you don't respond to the book, you're not a citizen. That sounds crazy— and it makes perfect sense if you see the story in the book as an inevitable, fated account of what it means to be American, and to live up to the charge in the American charter.

How does this transference in culture, a transference that creates a common conversation, happen? It happens when a story is made up that feels as if it were always there, so that both the shock and the pleasure of recognition is present when even the most stray fragment invades the day, diverts your contemplation of the news story you're reading ("a Gatsby-for-our-time," George Will wrote of Donald Trump's inauguration), the movie you're watching, the political speech you're listening to, and just like that brings the whole—the whole story, the whole of the common imagination, the very idea that there is such a thing—into view. How that happens with *The Great Gatsby* is the subject of this book, but how it happened with another book—one written well before but in cultural time first making itself felt at about the same time that Fitzgerald's book appeared—may be a place to start. It's a book that, in America, defines the contours of a common imagination as much as anything America has ever produced, though in 1925— when after the wild commercial success of *This Side of Paradise* in 1920 and the vastly greater literary success of *The Beautiful and Damned* in 1922, *The Great Gatsby* did not sell and its failure was not mourned by reviewers, as the failure of the earlier book almost seventy-five years before had not been mourned—it had barely any place in the American imagination at all. Its sails had been lowered for nearly three quarters of a century, but all that time they were taking on wind and storing energy. When the pages were finally opened again—thanks in great part to Raymond Weaver's *Herman Melville: Mariner and Mystic* in 1921 and D. H. Lawrence's *Studies in Classic American Literature* in 1923—it was not long before the book could seem as if it were a founding document, to be placed alongside the Declaration of Independence, the Constitution, and "The Battle Hymn of the Republic," or anyway listed in *TV Guide* in 1961. "*Moby Dick*. 116 min. Gregory Peck, Richard Basehart,

Orson Welles. A mad captain enlists others in his quest to kill a white whale."

Just as you can with *"The Great Gatsby* is about the efforts of this one man, Jay Gatsby, to reinvent himself"—the first sentence in the voice-over narration to the SparkNotes cartoon video of the book—you can look at the *TV Guide* listing and stop on that dime. Isn't that America, the thing itself, right there? "I, Ishmael, was one of that crew; my shouts had gone up with the rest; my oath had been welded with theirs; and stronger I shouted, and more did I hammer and clinch my oath, because of the dread in my soul. A wild, mystical, sympathetical feeling was in me; Ahab's quenchless feud seemed mine." So said Ishmael, after Ahab's appearance on the quarterdeck of the *Pequod* to charge the crew: "I'll chase him round Good Hope, and round the Horn, and round the Norway Maelstrom, and round perdition's flames before I give him up. And this is what ye have shipped for, men! to chase that white whale on both sides of land, and over all sides of earth, till he spouts black blood and rolls fin out. What say ye, men, will ye splice hands on it, now?"

"Is it that by its indefiniteness it shadows forth the heartless voids and immensities of the universe, and thus stabs us from behind with the thought of annihilation, when beholding the white depths of the milky way?" Ishmael reflects on the white whale, the sea for the moment eddying quietly up against the hull. "Or is it, that as in essence whiteness is not so much a color as the visible absence of color, and at the same time the concrete of all colors; is it for these reasons that there is such a dumb blankness, full of meaning, in a white landscape of snows—a colorless, all-color of atheism from which we shrink?" Do we even need to hear these voices?

In our imagination, as if not even a particular author was ever needed, in the American story Ahab is always out there, with the whale ahead of him and Ishmael always along for the ride. Here he is by way of the ubiquitous Edmund Wilson, writing on Grant in *Patriotic Gore* the year after the *TV Guide* listing: "I do not want to add to the bizarre interpretations already offered for *Moby-Dick* by suggesting that it anticipates the Civil War, but"—and then he is off, at first starting slowly ("there are moments, in reading the *Memoirs*, when one is reminded of Captain Ahab's quest"), and then carried forward as if by the force of the story itself, as if the story itself were history, Ahab in pursuit of Moby Dick, Ulysses S. Grant in pursuit of Robert E. Lee, the first story, not the second, the real history the country has made, or has always listened for—the story it has always needed to tell. Quickly Wilson is on to Grant's pages on how the world made Lee into a mystical figure whose victories are miraculous and his escapes no less so (Grant: "The number of his forces was always lowered and that of the National forces exaggerated"), and, while not wanting to add to any bizarre interpretations, arranging the props on stage ("We look forward to the eventual encounter as to the final scene of a drama—as we wait for the moment when Ahab, stubborn, intent and tough, crippled by his wooden leg as Grant had sometimes been by his alcoholic habits, will confront the smooth and shimmering foe, who has so far eluded all hunters"). Here in Wilson's steps is the novelist E. L. Doctorow, in 2007, addressing a rant called "The White Whale" to a joint meeting of the American Academy of Arts and Sciences and the American Philosophical Society, Doctorow as a devious-cruising *Rachel* coming across the black carcass of a butchered sperm whale ("It will take more than revelations of an inveterately corrupt Administration to dissolve the miasma of otherworldly weirdness hanging over this land"), then trying to find solid ground as the ship pitches on the sea ("Melville in *Moby-Dick* speaks of reality outracing apprehension . . . reality as too much for us to take in, as, for example, the white whale is too much for the Pequod and its captain. It may be that our new century is an awesomely complex white whale"), but the white whale looms up only to disappear and reappear ("It would be good for Utah," the *Salt Lake Tribune* announced in an editorial at the end of 2017, "if Hatch, having finally caught the Great White Whale of tax reform, were to call it a career. If he doesn't, the voters should end it for him"),* now a new century, now the Constitution and the great white buildings it built, now America's enemy as Doctorow sights it. For one who does not want to add to the bizarre interpretations already offered for *Moby-Dick*, it is a relief to come back down to earth, open the book itself, and read, perhaps in the

---

* "The selection of Sen. Orrin G. Hatch as the 2017 Utahn of the Year has little to do with the fact that, after 42 years, he is the longest-serving Republican senator in U.S. history, that he has been a senator from Utah longer than three-fifths of the state's population has been alive. It has everything to do with recognizing Hatch's part in the dramatic dismantling of the Bears Ears and Grand Staircase-Escalante national monuments—His role as chairman of the Senate Finance Committee in passing a major overhaul of the nation's tax code—His utter lack of integrity that rises from his unquenchable thirst for power."

fall of 2004, or 2008, or 2012, or 2016, or 2020, in its first chapter, these prosaic words:

> *"Grand Contested Election for the Presidency*
> *of the United States"*
> "WHALING VOYAGE BY ONE ISHMAEL"
> "BLOODY BATTLE IN AFFGHANISTAN"

Is any of that even needed? Do we need Melville sitting in his house in Pittsfield, Massachusetts, writing to Nathaniel Hawthorne in November of 1851, when Melville was thirty-two, "A sense of unspeakable security is in me this moment, on account of your having understood the book," or thinking back on that day forty years later, the year he died, he not only the only one to remember it, but the only one left who might care? Is, today, the book even needed? As James Conant has written, "Certain forms of speech seem not to require recovery, because they seem to have always been with us and are everywhere still with us"—"what matters," as Harold Bloom wrote in 2002, more than three decades after the music of the shades who once traded under the names Rick Danko, Levon Helm, Garth Hudson, Richard Manuel, and Robbie Robertson was first heard, "is that the songs at their best seem always to have been there, until refined by The Band,"* which is why the opening lines

---

* The songs, Bloom went on, pressing his idea of place as knowledge, "express the North American loneliness, with its related malaise that no American feels free if she or he is not alone. . . . A nihilistic and anarchic quasi-mysticism is endemic in their music. There is, as I have argued elsewhere, a post-Protestant gnosis in North America, which

of "The Weight" can sound like Ishmael's account of falling in line at funeral processions—

> I pulled into Nazareth
> Was feeling 'bout half past dead
> I just need some place
> Where I can lay my head
> Hey Mister, can you tell me
> Where a man might find a bed
> He just grinned and shook his head
> No was all he said

—and why Ishmael's account of Ahab's speech comes out in the cadence of a jeremiad: it was already there. The book reads the culture and the culture reads the book: thus one might open the paper on a Friday morning, scan the listings, and find this triple bill at a place called the Great American Music Hall: "Or, the Whale, the Federalists, and Emily Jane White." As Ishmael mused, just before offering his trio of headlines: "And, doubtless, my going on this whaling voyage, formed part of the grand programme of Providence that was drawn up a long time ago. It came in as a sort of brief interlude

---

could be called 'the American Religion.' The Band's performances . . . seem to emanate directly from that gnosis, as the Dylan of 1965–75 seemed to also. If our freedom is our solitude, it is also our wavering sense that what is best and oldest in us is no part of the creation. A spirituality that unsponsored has its sorrows, some of which The Band caught and rendered permanently."

and solo between more extensive performances. I take it that this part of the bill must have run something like this."

Lines from a book or essay I will never pin down stick in my mind: *There they are, year after year, the drunks in the White Horse holding up the bar to shout out the last lines of "The Great Gatsby."* If only because it has been done to death, the last sentence of *The Great Gatsby* may be the most famous ending in American literature. Melville came up with the most famous opening line in American literature, in the American tall tale, in the American shaggy dog story. It's quick, it's fast, it comes at you like a man extending his hand and pulling it back before you have a chance to grasp it: *No was all he said.* It contains all possibilities. When, some years ago, I saw a CALL ME ISHMAEL bumper sticker on a car in Oakland, California, it didn't occur to me that it was a souvenir of someone's visit to the Melville museum in Pittsfield; I figured it was something the all-American novelist and Oaklander Ishmael Reed had made up for himself.

Why is it not a cliché? Because it rings a bell, because the line snaps back like a boom? Or because it speaks for the American as a creature of disguise and self-invention, each one an embodiment of his or her own country, fated to act out its drama in his or her own skin? John Smith, James van Sciver, Sergius O'Shaughnessy, Frederick Douglass, Jimmy Gatz, Vito Corleone, Billy Blythe, Asa Yoelson, Dick Whitman, Fritz Schneider—any of these could be the name Ishmael is hiding. "Call me Ishmael" means we will never know what it is.

Past Fitzgerald's for *The Great Gatsby* there are many great endings in American literature, as if the country's most poetic stories incline toward the end of America, that idea contained whole in the skin of a single character, as an explicit or hidden charge. These endings are always political, whatever their costuming in private dramas; no matter what passport the reader might carry, they momentarily implicate the reader as an American. As with *The Great Gatsby* and its Dutch sailors' vanishing vision. As with Fitzgerald's *Tender Is the Night*, with Dick Diver somewhere in upstate New York, "like Grant in Galena," waiting to be called. As with Philip Roth's *I Married a Communist*, with all of those the story has consumed living on forever as burning stars in the sky, each his or her own furnace:

> Neither the ideas of their era nor the expectations of our species were determining destiny: hydrogen alone was determining destiny. There are no longer mistakes for Eve or Ira to make. There is no betrayal. There is no idealism. There are no falsehoods. There is neither conscience nor its absence. There are no mothers and daughters, no fathers and stepfathers. There are no actors. There is no class struggle. There is no discrimination or lynching or Jim Crow, nor has there ever been. There is no injustice, nor is there justice. There are no utopias.

Roth doesn't say "There is no America." Somehow, given the story *Moby-Dick* has already told, Roth's cosmology of negation can't negate that—because the ending of *Moby-Dick* trumps all other endings, and seems to have been written to do nothing less. Under the red white and blue? Ahab killed by the whale, the *Pequod* smashed by the whale and sinking into its own vortex, pulling down every man and boat, and as the last mast is about to disappear below the surface there is the "red arm and a hammer" of the harpooner Tashtego, the Gay Head American Indian from Martha's Vineyard. His arm "hovered backwardly uplifted in the open air, in the act of nailing the flag faster and yet faster to the subsiding spar. A sky-hawk that tauntingly had followed the main-truck downwards from its natural home among the stars, pecking at the flag, and incommoding Tashtego there; this bird now chanced to intercept its broad fluttering wing between the hammer and the wood; and simultaneously feeling that ethereal thrill, the submerged savage beneath, in his death-gasp, kept his hammer frozen there"—a scene that John Huston, filming *Moby-Dick* in 1956, did not even try to shoot. The last chapters of the book are an action movie, a nineteenth-century version of Steve McQueen's car chase in *Bullitt*, and though, as befitting the nineteenth century, when everything was slower and simpler, "The Chase" lasts three days,* the action is so furious that, for the final scene, as you read, Melville's symbolism doesn't even begin to work as such. This is actually happening. You can't believe it as you watch. You can't believe you're alive to tell this tale.

In every way, to read *Moby-Dick* is to reread it. As with *The Great Gatsby*, there is something there that, as another writer

---

* As "The Chase: The First Day," "The Chase: The Second Day," and "The Chase: The Third Day." On YouTube you can find the ten-and-a-half minute *Bullitt* sequence as "The Chase (Part One)," "The Chase (Part Two)," and "The Chase (Part Three)."

has put it, speaking of "Verdi's arias, various blues songs, certain poems," gives the sense that "the creator came upon them by accident and we are, for the first time, discovering them for him." Given the diffusion and the presence of *Moby-Dick* and its metaphors, any time one sits down with the book, even if it's for the first time, the act carries with it a sense of return. One can forget so much of what's there, with hardly a phrase needed to bring a hundred pages back to mind in an instant. There is the way almost the entire first section of the book, until the *Pequod* sets sail, is a nonstop comedy, Ishmael first as Bob Hope in *Road to Utopia*, then as Abbott running an outrageous who's-on-first routine with his New Bedford innkeeper Costello, then Ishmael's one-night stand with the tattooed Queequeg turning into at least a two-night marriage—but not before proving, in a set of syllogisms so satisfyingly precise you don't even care where they're leading, that it is a Christian's duty to worship a pagan idol. There is the language, sometimes stopping the book cold in its own pages ("He looked like a man cut away from the stake," Ishmael says of Ahab when he first sees him, and what Appalachian murder ballad was that line from, or waiting for?), often so free-swinging that its slang leaps from its time to ours without slipping a step into obsolescence: "Give it up, subsubs!" "Who ain't a slave?" "Cool as an icicle." There is the thrill of keeping up with a writer who moves so fast that you pull up short to catch your breath and wonder how he gets from a deckhand knocked around by a boss to the "universal thump" of democratic comradeship ("all hands should rub each other's shoulder-blades") in a paragraph. The rhetoric and the ethos of Jacksonian democracy, often taken to Olympian heights, make the wind behind so many of

Ishmael's musings, but still — how does Melville move Ishmael from his ardor over Ahab casting thunderbolts on the quarterdeck to an analysis of the captain and his mates that could pass for an editorial in the *Democratic Review* on the flaws of Millard Fillmore's cabinet specifically and the state of the nation generally? "Here, then," our tour guide tells us, "was this grey-headed, ungodly old man, chasing with curses a Job's whale round the world, at the head of a crew, too, chiefly made up of mongrel renegades, and castaways, and cannibals — morally enfeebled also, by the incompetence of mere unaided virtue or right-mindedness in Starbuck, the invulnerable jollity of indifference and recklessness in Stubb, and the pervading mediocrity in Flask."

Even without reading the book, even with only a *TV Guide* sense of the story, you're rereading the book when you're flipping channels and chance on John Wayne's Thomas Dunson in *Red River*, a movie made in 1948, or for that matter Robert Mitchum's preacher Harry Powell in *Night of the Hunter*, from 1955, which was a better movie version of *Moby-Dick* than *Moby Dick*.* You're rereading it if you recall Elvis Presley in 1968 facing the white faces of his audience for the first time in seven years and against the blank-

---

* And flipping channels, you can even find yourself subliminally rereading the book, as when you come across an episode of a Dean Martin show from somewhere in the ether of the 1960s, and discover that as Nick Tosches once put it, "Ajax was no longer a Homeric hero; he was the *Comedy Hour*'s sponsor's foaming cleanser, no longer a contender with Odysseus for the arms of Achilles, but a consort of Fab, which had itself transplanted Melville's musings on 'The Whiteness of the Whale' with the dictum 'Whiter Whites without Bleaching.'"

ness of that unknown hoisting a microphone stand like a harpoon, thrusting it over the crowd, and shouting "Moby Dick!" You are rereading if you're watching a young black boy, one Woody, as an early incarnation of Bob Dylan and a latter-day incarnation of Melville's cabin-boy Pip, pitched out of a boxcar by hobo thugs and into a river, only to see a sperm whale guiding toward him in the 2007 film *I'm Not There*, or going back to the TV for a rerun of the 2008 episode of *Law & Order: Criminal Intent* where the tormented police detective Bobby Goren comes face to face with the unmistakable handiwork of the escaped serial killer Nicole Wallace, once a sham literature professor whose specialty was Melville. She lectures in flashback: "The descent into madness is usually preceded by obsession. What characterizes Ahab's obsession? I always fancied it was man's unrelenting pursuit of his own potency." "I'm told she's your white whale," Goren's boss says to him, just before Goren receives a card postmarked Pittsfield, Massachusetts. When, early on in the book, Captain Peleg asks Ishmael, "Want to see what whaling is, eh? Have ye clapped eye on Captain Ahab?" and Ishmael answers "Who is Captain Ahab, sir?" we're surprised he hasn't heard of him; we have.

Writers have their unspoken ambitions. Did Melville hope, or even know, that his countrymen and women would always seek out the mysteries that, in his big book, the book that would for the rest of his life erase his once-famous name from the memories of his fellow citizens, he took down as if they were the plainest, most obvious facts, himself the sub-sub-librarian he so confidently laughed off? That famous letter from Hawthorne, the letter in which he showed Melville that he "understood the book," the letter that, presumably, deciphered the book's true, transcendent meaning, so we would not have to *ask*, the letter that, unlike Melville's response to Hawthorne, does not survive—it could have been one of Poe's hoaxes, were he still around in 1851 to forge it, a trick to keep the characters alive, running their histories through history still unmade, unmaking history as they left it behind and continued on their way.

What did Hawthorne say? No, Melville may not have kept letters, as Hawthorne did, but one can imagine a ceremony a little more to the point than taking out the trash. "Cool as an icicle," as Ishmael says of Queequeg sitting among the other harpooners in the Spouter-Inn, his harpoon in hand, "reaching over the table with it, to the imminent jeopardy of many heads, and grappling the beefsteaks towards him. But *that* was certainly very coolly done by him, and every one knows that in most people's estimation, to do anything coolly is to do it genteelly." So how cool, how genteel it was for Melville, sitting in his writing room late at night, with no one to glimpse a single word when he burned the pages.

Fitzgerald wasn't cool. His correspondence on *The Great Gatsby* to and from his editor Maxwell Perkins, sometimes proud, more often nervous—he's twenty-eight, it's his third novel, the first the career-making hit, the second not as big but far better, and this has to be bigger and better still—is floundering and sterile. "Among a set of characters marvelously palpable and vital—I would know Tom Buchanan if I met him on the street and would avoid him—Gatsby is somewhat vague," Perkins wrote in November of 1924 when he first saw the manuscript. "The reader's eyes can never quite focus upon him, his outlines are dim. . . . Couldn't *he* be physically described as distinctly as the others, and couldn't you add one or two characteristics like the use of that phrase 'old sport,'—not verbal, but physical ones, perhaps." Later he says the reader has to know where Gatsby's money came from and why he seems older than he's supposed to be. *And really, what does he look like?* Fitzgerald writes back: his "first instinct" is to throw out Gatsby and make the book about Tom Buchanan ("I suppose he's the best character I've ever done," he writes incomprehensibly of the polo-playing thug who may be among the ten richest men in America. "—and I think he and the brother in 'Salt' & Hurstwood in 'Sister Carrie' are the three best characters in American fiction in the last twenty years"). They try to bring Gatsby into focus ("*I myself didn't know what Gatsby looked like or was engaged in,*" Fitzgerald writes in the same letter, but "after having had Zelda draw pictures until her fingers ache I know Gatsby better than I know my own child"), but the character fades as you read the letters. If, as Fitzgerald describes Gatsby on the second page of his novel, "personality is an unbroken series of successful gestures," then personality is a chimera and Gatsby was never there at all. Reading this letter, you can believe Fitzgerald's boast to the novelist Thomas Boyd six months before: "I shall write a novel better than any novel ever written in America and become par excellence the best second-rater in the world."

READING THE BOOK

I can say for sure I didn't understand it in high school. I felt I understood it, that's the big problem. That's the biggest obstacle to understanding, is thinking that you understand. So, with "Gatsby," you think you got it, especially as a young person. And somehow things keep getting emphasized—Jazz Age, opulence, elegance, blah blah blah, vivacity—so you think that's what it's about, it's about the Jazz Age or something. But I didn't understand at all that, and he states it explicitly—and that's why you have to listen and so much is revealed—it's about outsiders and Midwesterners, he says this is a book about the Middle West.

—*Jim Fletcher, quoted in Gazelle Emami and Mallika Rao, "'Gatz' Interview: The 6-hour-Plus, Word-for-Word Performance of 'The Great Gatsby,'"* Huffington Post, *April 12, 2012*

White genocide is a white nationalist belief that white people, as a race, are endangered and face extinction as a result of nonwhite immigration and marriage between the races, a process being manipulated by Jews. . . . It is the underlying concept behind far-right, anti-immigration arguments, especially those aimed at immigrants who are not white Christians. The concept was popularized by Bob Whitaker, a former economics professor and Reagan appointee to the Office of Personnel Management, who wrote a 221-word "mantra" on the subject that ended with the rallying cry: "Anti-racist is code word for anti-white." . . . The concept of white genocide was often communicated through a white supremacist saying called the Fourteen Words: "We must secure the existence of our people and a future for white children." The saying was created by David Lane, a white supremacist sentenced to 190 years in prison in connection with the 1984 murder of the Jewish radio host Alan Berg.

—*Liam Stack, "Alt-Right, Alt-Left, Antifa: A Glossary of Extremist Language," New York Times, August 15, 2017*

"A giant pair of blue eyes rose over Grand Avenue Sunday in St. Paul, peering out of gold-colored spectacles onto one of the city's most popular shopping and dining corridors.

"Spelled out beneath the spectral eyes are the words: 'Doctor T. J. Eckleburg. Oculist.'

"The 500-pound, 9-foot-tall, and 17-foot-long steel sign stopped some pedestrians in their tracks. One woman asked: 'Is he fictional?'

"Tom Mischke beamed. It was exactly the 'what-on-earth?' reaction he spent 20 years trying to bring to St. Paul to honor author F. Scott Fitzgerald and his best-known novel.

"'What would make you open "The Great Gatsby" more?' Mischke later asked. 'A statue of him? Or a weird sign from the book?'

"The piece of public art replicates a billboard mentioned several times in Fitzgerald's novel. The eyes often are interpreted as emblematic of God peering down and perhaps passing judgment.

"Its origin story started with Mischke, a local writer, musician and radio host who was trying to persuade his friend, David Ulrich, to open a business on Grand Avenue and install a Fitzgerald tribute. But Ulrich, owner of the Spectacle Shoppe, had locations in Minneapolis and elsewhere.

"'I didn't think I needed it,' Ulrich said of a St. Paul location.

"Mischke, a lifelong St. Paul resident bent on honoring one of the city's most well-known natives, was relentless. 'I wouldn't just ask him once a year,' Mischke said. 'I'd ask him several times a year.'

"Ulrich opened his St. Paul location on Grand Avenue near Lexington Avenue about five years ago, and in the spring of 2017 gave his blessing for the sign.

"To sweeten the project, Mischke timed its installation Sunday to coincide with Fitzgerald's 121st birthday. 'The average person may not be aware that this went up on Fitzgerald's birthday, but I'll always know that, that this was a gift to this guy's memory,' Mischke said. 'I feel like it's the least I can do for the gift of that book.'" — Chao Xiong, "Eye candy? Art on Grand Ave. honors St. Paul native F. Scott Fitzgerald," *Minneapolis Star-Tribune*, September 25, 2017

In the last half-hour of the March 8, 1978, episode of *Saturday Night Live*, Andy Kaufman, a frequent guest on the show, appeared for his final segment of the night. Dressed in tails, he came onto a stage bare except for a phonograph box on a table. He opened the box and the sound of a patriotic fanfare came out; in a fulsomely phony British accent, every syllable an éclair, he announced to the audience that since there were only twenty minutes left on the show, and because he'd been on so many times before, "they told me, the producers, the people who run the show said they trusted me very much, and they would let me do whatever I want, I could have the rest of the time, if it takes that long—so, I was wondering what to do." He runs through the various shtick characters he plays, ponders singing a song, doing a dance, and then, he says, he noticed a book—*booook*, it comes out, his accent taking on more ballast, more loam, with every new thought. "It was lying, just a little while ago, it was lying around," he says, "and it reminded me of when I was in school, and this literature teacher gave me this book, told me to read it, and said it was the greatest American novel ever written. And, ah, I take issue with that. I don't believe that it is, but what I'd like to do, I'd like to read it to you—and then perhaps you could point out some subtleties I might have missed—in case, you know, if we have time to follow, for a discussion."

He picks a paperback off the table. "It's called *The Great Gatsby*. It's by F. Scott Fitzgerald. And, here it is—" And he begins: "'Chapter one.'" He looks as if he's about to embark on a distasteful but somehow necessary task.

"'In my younger and more vulnerable years my father gave me some advice that I've been turning over in my mind ever since,'" he reads, his orotund tone holding, but flatly. "'"Whenever you feel like criticizing any one," he told me'"—and you begin to realize these may be the dullest first lines of a novel you've ever encountered—"It was a dark and stormy night" now sounds inspired— "'"just remember that all the people in this world haven't had the advantages that you've had."'"

People begin laughing. They know this one. They're right back in high school. "'He didn't say any more,'" Kaufman picks up, with *didn't say any more* bringing even more laughter, as if Kaufman has just dropped a clue that in a few moments he won't say any more, "'but we've always been unusually communicative in a reserved way'"—and this is really boring, this is almost stupefyingly boring, this is not "Call me Ishmael. Some years ago—never mind how long precisely," where Melville has you on the hook right there, wanting to know what he's concealing—and now people are starting to crack up. Kaufman goes on—and just when he gets to "'In consequence, I'm inclined to reserve all judgments, a habit that has opened up many curious natures to me and also made me the victim of not a few veteran bores,'" the word *bores* echoes in the crowd like a little bomb. One unseen person in particular seems to be coming apart.

Kaufman reads faster, and the people are laughing more, and then they stop, as if realizing that he's not stopping. There is booing. There are groans. There are unpleasant grumbles. There's a feeling of revolt: "NO!" someone shouts. Kaufman makes a slight adjustment: now, at the beginning of each sentence, there's a tiny pause, each one containing at least the suggestion that he might stop, and with each pause the noise jumps. The boos and shouts of NO! are loud and constant. He's only on page two. He has been reading for little more than a minute.

There is hectoring, anger, laughter when Kaufman merely emphasizes a line. He's drowned out. He licks his lips, and turns a page with an expression that with his fat tone says, *This is quite terrible, isn't it? Pretentious.* He pauses; the crowd senses an opening and rushes through it and begins to shout as a body. "'When I came back from the East last autumn,'" Kaufman goes on, now seeming more engaged in the book, picking up a certain intellectual momentum—but the crowd has taken over. "Now, look," he says, "let's keep it—down, please, because you know we have a long way to go." For a moment everyone laughs. Then the hectoring starts up again. "Look," Kaufman says, "we're pressed for time—if you don't mind. 'When I came back from the East last autumn,'" he begins again. There is an eruption of dismay. "'I felt that I wanted the world to be in uniform and at a sort of moral attention forever; I wanted no more riotous excursions with privileged glimpses into the human heart'"—this *is* interesting, the words may not immediately explain themselves but the feeling of dislocation they give off has a hint of sulfur, but no one is listening. "'Only Gatsby,'" Kaufman continues directly, pointing a finger in the air, "'the man who gives his name to this book, was exempt from my reaction— Gatsby'"—and now there's a big, rolling boo, like the Wave at a ballpark, saying, *Enough.*

"No, no, now wait a minute, right now," Kaufman says, his dark eyes piercing the crowd. "Hold on. If I hear any *more*—I want it quiet. If I hear *one more* sound I'm going to *close* this book and forget the whole thing." Everyone cheers and applauds. Kaufman looks surprised. "All right," he says. "Thank you very much. Thank you." He opens the book again. Someone shouts something abusive from the side: "*LEAVE THAT BOOK—*" "All right, that's it," Kaufman says. "You've made your bed, now lie in it. I'm going, that's it, good night." He begins to walk off; the audience applauds. He turns around, raising his arms in a gesture of reconciliation. "No, I'm only fooling," he says with a happy grin. "I wouldn't do that to you, no." He opens the book. "'Only *Gatsby*,'" the finger now back in the air, "'the man who gives his name to this book'"—there's good-natured laughter—"'Gatsby, who represented everything for which I have an unaffected scorn,'" and again the last word sparks its match in disdain from the crowd. "'If personality is an unbroken series of successful gestures—'"

The response crosses into fury. Kaufman is nonplussed. "Now, let me tell you something," he says pleasantly. "I think what we need nowadays is more discipline. When I was your age"—and he's quieted the crowd, and with his tony accent still in place, no one sees this old saw coming—"I used to have to walk about seven miles to school. Spare the rod and spoil the child is what I say—good half-hour in the woodshed would do some of you good." He scowls. The crowd is silent. He raises the book; there are more groans, now sounding almost defeated. "'If personality is a series—'" There is a torrent of boos and shouts. "What do you want me to do?" Kaufman says, suddenly disarmed. "Dance!" shouts a woman. "All right, good," he says. "'Only *Gatsby*—If personality is an unbroken series of successful gestures, then there was something gorgeous about him—'"

Lorne Michaels, the producer, rushes out from the back of the stage, puts one hand on Kaufman's shoulder, grasps his arm with the other. He whispers in Kaufman's ear, then rushes off. "I've been asked to leave," Kaufman says, visibly holding in his anger. "All right, *that's it*, ladies and gentlemen." The crowd cheers. "I have been asked to leave! And I resent it! I was told I could take all the time I wanted—now they ask me to leave. I was going to read this book, and then I was going to play you the music record"—he gestures toward the box on the table. "But that's it. You didn't want it, then fine, I won't even do that! No! You don't want the record either, do you?"—and at this point is there even a question of sanctity, of the redemptive power of art, of which cover on the book is

permitted or shameful? Isn't this something that belongs to everyone, something people can bat back and forth like a beach ball at
a Neil Young show?

There is a hubbub of shouts. Kaufman is encouraged. "How
many people want the record? How many people?" There are furious cheers. "All right. Do you really want the record?" "YES!" "Do
you really want the record? Or would you rather that I leave?" More
cheers. "All right, I'll do the record"—and he makes a show of contempt. "But, but, but *first*—the book." There is laughter. Kaufman
holds up his hand for silence. "Do you want the record?" There is
wild approval. "All right, we have the record—no, but—enough is
enough." He lifts the tone arm on the phonograph and drops the
stylus on the record. There is a loud, rolling opening groove. The
record begins to skip. Kaufman stands pompously erect, as if listening to the ocean's roar. "'Only Gatsby,'" the record begins in Kaufman's voice, "'the man who gives his name to this book—'"

This is where *Gatz*, the more-than-six-hour theatrical-group
word-for-word reading-recital-channeling of *The Great Gatsby*—
including breaks, a production lasting nearly eight hours—began.
John Collins, the founder of the downtown New York theater group
Elevator Repair Service (he took a career placement test once; elevator repairman came back), saw Kaufman's routine. He may have
felt cheated, as anyone can—by the time Kaufman stops, he has
established the book, and you want him to keep going. But what if
you could really do it?

As the director, Collins and different actors began to work-
shop the idea in a dingy, empty office in 1999, fifteen years after

Andy Kaufman's death from lung cancer at thirty-five. The setting seemed right so they kept it. Rights conflicts with the Fitzgerald estate limited any public performances to two- or three-hour open rehearsals in Brooklyn in 2004 and SoHo in 2005; in 2006 Collins was able to secure permission to stage the entire piece in Europe. Later that year the American premiere took place at the Walker Art Center in Minneapolis—only two weeks after the close of the world premiere of the work the estate was betting on, the director Simon Levy's straight dramatic adaptation of the book as *The Great Gatsby* at the Guthrie Theater in Minneapolis, which was aiming for Broadway but never made it. At the Walker the Collins work ran first in two parts over two days, then with both parts, with an hour break for dinner, on the same day, twice. It opened at the Public Theater in New York four years after that, was performed there again in 2019, and such a dull, boilerplate, nodding-off summary might be a useful way to set the stage that *Gatz* establishes: a flat, confined picture of for what drama its setting might be the setting. As useful boilerplate, as set down in a preview of the Simon Levy play by Mary Ann Grossmann in the *St. Paul Pioneer Press*, it sounds so outdated, so precious, so right for a thankfully lost silent movie melodrama—no setting for any drama at all, as with "The narrator is Nick Carraway, a young man from a middle-western city who goes East in 1922. He visits his cousin, Daisy, married to rich and unfeeling Tom Buchanan. And he meets Jay Gatsby, his wealthy and mysterious neighbor who had an affair with Daisy before he went into the military. Gatsby, who has longed for Daisy the entire time they were separated, was born James Gatz in North

Dakota. He made a lot of money as a bootlegger, re-invented himself and bought his castle on Long Island so he could reclaim Daisy.

"Nick also learns that Tom Buchanan is having an affair with Myrtle, the wife of an auto mechanic who lives in the Valley of Ashes, a colorless place dominated by the huge eyes of Dr. T. J. Eckleburg, an image on an old billboard.

"After a confrontation in a New York City hotel, during which Daisy says she loves Gatsby and Tom, Daisy accidentally runs over Myrtle while driving Gatsby's car. Myrtle's husband shoots Gatsby and then himself. Nick decides the East 'is haunted for me' and returns to the Midwest."

As *Gatz* played for the first time in full in the United States, on September 23, 2006, the curtain went up on a grubby office. A table in the middle of the room with chairs at either end serves as a double desk, with a typewriter at the left end and a computer at the right—a big, dirty-looking computer that along with a bulky cordless phone places the time in a dead corner of the 1980s. There's a back door and a window in the back wall, and behind it a hallway; on the far left in the back of the room there's an enclosure for an office manager—Lucille, played in the Walker production by Kate Scelsa. There's a couch behind the desk and file cabinets on the right side of the room. Nick, played by Scott Shepherd—a blondish, nondescript sort of man, hazily small-town midwestern in his footsteps, maybe in his thirties, wearing a blue shirt, a patterned tie, dark pants—comes into the office carrying a takeout coffee. He takes off his jacket, hangs it up on a coat rack, and tries to start his computer. It doesn't start; he doesn't seem surprised. He can't do anything until it's fixed. You see Lucille make a call.

Shepherd idly flips open a Rolodex box and sees a dog-eared paperback in it. He picks it up, sits down in a chair, and starts reading out loud. He's got time to kill. In the audience, because you've read about the play and bought a ticket, you already know the book is *The Great Gatsby*, but in the miasma of the setting nothing quite connects. The vaguely *Twilight Zone* ambience further dissipates whatever recognition you might have brought to the motions the Shepherd character seems to be going through. It's one thing for Andy Kaufman to tell you a set-up story about seeing a book lying around somewhere, just so he can get into his routine. It's another to see someone doing exactly what you might do in the same circumstance: pick up something to read, anything, a book, a magazine, even a company newsletter, because you don't have anything else to do.

Jim, Nick's office mate, maybe his nominal boss, played by Jim Fletcher, comes in. He's bald, stolid, tall, slightly bulky, in his forties, maybe fifty, dressed in a pale jacket, blue shirt, a tie that matches Nick's but darker. He carries himself like a city midwesterner, a *Main Street* character too minor to have a name. He has the charisma of his desk chair. He takes off his jacket and sits down. The phone rings: Nick picks it up, still reading out loud as he listens to the voice on the other end, and hands the phone to Jim, who taps on the back of Nick's computer to shush him. Holding the book in his left hand, as he will do for more than six hours, the office room and its furniture doing double-time for raucous party scenes with paper flying through the air and everyone drunk, for hotel or cottage scenes frozen with tension or breaking down in slapstick, for cars and trains and a cemetery, Nick randomly taps keys on his computer. With a surreptitious turn of his head, as if he's getting away with something, he softens his tone against Jim's phone conversation but keeps reading.

Lucille comes out of her cubicle and hands Jim a paper to sign. She looks at Nick reading as if he's a little nuts. Tom—a maintenance man with keys on his belt played by Robert Cucuzza, is seen in the enclosure. An office worker cast as "The Golf Specialist"—Fitzgerald's golf champion and Daisy Buchanan confidant Jordan Baker, played by Susie Sokol in a white polo shirt, dark slacks, and white canvas shoes—comes in, moving up to Nick to read over his shoulder. Nick begins to read loudly in the voice of Tom Buchanan, playing him really, in a scratchy, unpleasant voice, as the golfer mugs and grossly mimics what a gross jerk this Tom Buchanan must be: there hasn't been a recognizable, arresting character to emerge out of Nick's mouth before this, including Nick Carraway. Except for someone on Fitzgerald's West Egg, Nick Carraway's déclassé Great Neck side of Manhasset Bay on Long Island, asking for directions—Nick, trying to learn the bond business on Wall Street, is renting a cottage next to a huge mansion "that rented for twelve or fifteen thousand a season"—these are the first lines of dialogue in the book, which is to say in *Gatz*. The golfer stretches out on the couch and starts reading a golf magazine. Tom comes into the room. You get the overwhelming feeling that there's actually no work done in this office.

An office worker named as "Tom's wife," a dark-haired woman in a cream skirt-and-sweater set, played by Tory Vazquez, who will start speaking as Daisy, shows up. Tom grabs her and pulls her into the enclosure where they can't be seen. She comes back out, throwing an angry look over her shoulder, and goes over to a cabinet to check files. Nick is reading on the couch—the pages where the Nick he hasn't yet become, the Nick Carraway of the book in his hand, has gone to the Buchanans' house on Fitzgerald's East Egg, the more fashionable, old-money Manhasset Neck, to see his cousin Daisy.

Nick reads in the person of Daisy.* In Shepherd's voice, she sounds like a woman with money and no reason to be born might sound if she were trying to get someone to pay attention to her. "It was the kind of voice that the ear follows up and down, as if each speech is an arrangement of notes that will never be played again" doesn't come across in Shepherd's voice, but later, after Daisy— Tom's wife now speaking her own dialogue—has confessed to Nick what a worthless marriage she's made, this does: "The instant her voice broke off, ceasing to compel my attention, my belief, I felt the basic insincerity of what she had said. It made me uneasy, as though the whole evening had been a trick of some sort to exact a contributory emotion from me. I waited, and sure enough, in a moment she looked at me with an absolute smirk on her lovely face, as if she had asserted her membership in a rather distinguished secret society to which she and Tom belonged." Here, with the physical presence of

---

* *Gatsby* quotations from "The Authorized Text," Scribner Paperback Fiction, 1995, the edition used by Elevator Repair Service. When Shepherd is reading from the text, normal quotes—"Hello"—are used. When he is quoting dialogue from himself or others, internal quotes— "'Goodbye'"—are used. When other actors speak their own dialogue, normal quotes are used.

the person who is going to carry you through the story, you might sense, as you may not as a reader, a foreshadowing of the end of the book, still more than seven hours away, of how, when it's all over, when the bodies have been counted off, Daisy and Tom "retreated back into their money or their vast carelessness or whatever it was that kept them together."

Lucille gives Nick a memo. The book never out of his hand, his lips never ceasing to move, he puts the memo in a filing cabinet. "Civilization's going to pieces," announces Tom, the maintenance man speaking in a mean, grating voice. Nick looks up startled. It's the first spoken voice of the story other than his own. Something is happening to the story he hasn't expected. It's a surprise to the audience, which isn't expecting another voice. And it's a displacement: this ordinary-looking guy with a harsh working-class accent isn't a big, smooth, ruling-class goon like Tom Buchanan, but he doesn't seem as stupid, either, even if he's doing a job that says Tom Buchanan's Yale, where Nick first knew him, isn't even a word to him. In a straight, arresting delivery, without any of Nick's affectations as Tom, he begins to recite his speech on *The Rise of the Colored Empires*, "by this man Goddard" that "everybody ought to read," acting, not reading, no book in his hand: "The idea is that if we don't look out the white race will be—will be utterly submerged. It's all scientific stuff; it's been proved . . . This idea is that we're Nordics. I am, and you are, and you are, and—" As Scott Shepherd picks up the novel's descriptive interruptions—"After an infinitesimal hesitation he included Daisy with a slight nod"—Tom stands still on the stage, impatient for his turn to start talking again. He comes back: "—and we've produced all the things that go to make civilization—oh, science and art, and all that. Do you see?"

More than when you simply read the book for yourself, to see and hear these words from an unexceptional working man who is speaking as a billionaire is to be startled out of the atmosphere of the book, of the grimy office stranded in time, to be startled into history. In 1925 Fitzgerald couldn't know that in less than fifteen years Tom Buchanan's white genocide theories would rule Europe and send millions to extermination, but in the twenties eugenics was all the rage among American intellectuals like Fitzgerald's friend Edmund Wilson. The pioneering scientific racism of such American eugenicists as Madison Grant, author of *The Passing of the Great Race*, from 1916, had a convulsive effect on Adolf Hitler, who read Grant and other American race intellectuals in prison in Germany in 1924, and for that matter sent them fan letters.* Even in 2006 or 2010, the people on the *Gatz* stage, as they spoke and listened to Tom Buchanan, couldn't have known that in a little more or a little less than a decade his words would herald fascist rallies in American cities and be echoed from the White House—but David Lane had promulgated his Fourteen Words well before Scott Shepherd first picked up *The Great Gatsby* and began to read it. Tom walks across the stage and hovers over Nick with an ugly, menacing

---

* Madison Grant's great champion was Maxwell Perkins of Scribner's, so famously the guiding hand for Fitzgerald, Ernest Hemingway, and Thomas Wolfe, who ensured that *The Passing of the Great Race* stayed in print throughout multiple editions.

presence that carries with it all of those things the audience knows and doesn't know are yet to come.

Something about the way the reading is set — the transfer of the novel from its milieu of riches to a milieu of office rent and take-out — gives rise to reflection as you watch, as you listen: you hear more, and more is going on. "Something was making him nibble at the edge of stale ideas," Nick says of Tom, but Fitzgerald's ear is attuned to something deeper. You can hear how alive Fitzgerald always was to clichés, how he understood how certain words or phrases became cant the instant they appeared. He heard how they emerged out of certain political imperatives to weaken speech and thought, to make even the notion of communicating difficult ideas dubious — as I write, under the already old but concrete clouds of *back in the day, it is what it is, the devil is in the details.* "The obvious phrase is simply not in it," Mencken wrote in his review of *The Great Gatsby*, whose plot he found ridiculously obvious; Fitzgerald understood how and why an artist would never use such phrases, not even ironically. He saw, as he perhaps wrote such a phrase and crossed it out, that it would dissolve any page that carried it and discredit any character that used it, discredit even the vileness of a character meant to be vile. It was the same ear for slang that, in the 1922 of the book, sounds deliciously, excitingly new, but would not date.

It's a choice or an instinct not to use words that were current as Fitzgerald wrote but that he could somehow sense would sound stale much earlier than a generation later. So nothing is swell in *The Great Gatsby.* There are no cat's pajamas, no bee's knees, no hotsy totsys. Nobody's jake — and "hard-boiled," "a really good idea," or "hated his guts" sound as much like real American speech nearly a hundred years later as they did nearly a hundred years ago. You can think, in the way an idea can take shape more quickly than any word can be spoken, that with that tough, blunt phrase "stale ideas" Fitzgerald was saying, behind Nick's voice, more than he seemed. It will all echo back in the end, in the hotel room in New York, as Tom takes Gatsby apart: "I suppose the latest thing is to sit back and let Mr. Nobody from Nowhere make love to your wife. . . . Nowadays people begin by sneering at family life and family institutions, and next they'll throw everything overboard and have intermarriage between black and white."

Put that way, Tom's ideas weren't remotely stale in 1922, and in the America of nearly a century later they would be empowered and armed. Fitzgerald's ear takes him to the reality of American speech, into a kind of bet, as he shaped the paragraph, letting out the narrator Nick's naïveté like someone feeding a worm to a snake, that in America such ideas will never be stale — any more than hard-boiled (it was his great-uncle who made his family's fortune, Nick says — "I never saw this great-uncle, but I'm supposed to look like him — with special reference to the rather hard-boiled painting that hangs in Father's office") will ever be dead. Eighty-four years later, for the detective novelist Walter Mosley, the phrase defined America as he defined the phrase: "To have faith is to be a fool."*

---

* "From our prisons to our ghettos, from our boardrooms to the Oval Office, from gangsta rap to the Patriot Act," Mosley wrote in 2009, "America is a hard-boiled nation. . . . If I were asked to define hardboiled language I would simply say that it is elegant and concise

The telephone rings in the office. Lucille comes out, picks up the phone and hands it to Tom, who goes into Lucille's enclosure to talk. In the book, as Nick reads, the telephone rings in the Buchanans' house. There's agitated talking from the enclosure. As Shepherd starts to read again Susie Sokol's golfer now steps up directly, speaking as Jordan: "Don't talk. I want to hear what happens." "'Is something happening?'" "I thought everybody knew," the golfer says, surprised Nick doesn't know Tom's taking a call from his girlfriend. As the Daisy Buchanan office worker and the Tom Buchanan maintenance man say their lines, with the pages of the book fluttering in Shepherd's hand, there is the sense that as the quickly spoken interjections from the people on the stage connect into a story, this is all a common memory, in the way that Lincoln delivering the Gettysburg Address is a common memory.

Everyone sits around the desk that has become the Buchanans' dinner table. Your eye goes to Tory Vazquez's Daisy, who has the manner of a matter-of-fact, middle-class suburban housewife. There's nothing sophisticated about her, which sets Daisy's bitter "Sophisticated—God, I'm sophisticated!" off like an idea cracking. The dinner party at the Buchanans' breaks up. Nick leaves the

---

language used to describe an ugly and possibly irredeemable world; that, in spite of this elegance, it is a blunt object intent upon assault and battery." As in the way one of the nine people present at Gatsby's funeral, the only one, save Nick, of the hundreds or thousands who drank Gatsby's wine and danced to his music, who showed up, throws off "The poor son-of-a-bitch" as he turns away. Fitzgerald doesn't say how he says it. He sets the scene, lets it play, stops it cold, and lets the words come out like a fist.

office; when he comes back everyone has left. This seems to be what he was waiting for; he reads in the dark.

That is the end of the first chapter of the novel, and the first part of the play. There is already a strong feeling that everything to come has been glimpsed, as through a window you physically register as you walk down the street but don't see. What is especially present, the outline of the sketch already clear and undeniable, only waiting to be filled in, is the fundamental refusal of Daisy and Tom to grasp the seriousness of life — to evince a hint of Fitzgerald's conviction, as he wrote to his daughter in 1940, the year he died of a heart attack, at forty-four, that "the thing that lies behind all great careers, from Shakespeare's to Abraham Lincoln's, and as far back as there are books to read" was "the sense that life is essentially a cheat and its conditions are those of defeat, and that the redeeming things are not 'happiness and pleasure' but the deeper satisfactions that come out of struggle" — and their vast carelessness over who will pay the price for that refusal. The production has already held up a mirror to the novel and the audience's memory of it—a reflection acted out in charades—as if even the last pages of the book have already been glimpsed.

Part two brings on Chester, a repairman in a bow tie played by Vin Knight. He puts on glasses that match the eyes of the billboard of Dr. Eckleburg that Nick is describing as he reads passages about the train he's taking to New York with Tom. George, who will become George Wilson, the car mechanic husband of Tom's mistress, played by Aaron Landsman and dressed as a grease monkey, comes in and detaches Nick's broken keyboard, leaves, comes back, and reattaches it. Tom's Girl, Myrtle Wilson as played by Laurena Allan, comes in as an office worker who's also in George's garage as Tom stops there with Nick to tell her to meet him at the train station to go to their love nest in New York. With the office room transformed by nothing but gesture and attitude into a party at Tom and Myrtle's apartment, a Fletcher Henderson record starts playing. Nick, reading, holding a liquor bottle, has to shout over the loud music and drunken talk. Another office worker, Catherine, Tom's Girl's sister, played by Annie McNamara, is the party in one, a glamorous, happy drunk with odd, spidery movements you squint to follow. Lucille and Chester fill out the crowd. You can feel the party turning bad—Nick is reading, everyone else is acting noisily, yelling as if to prove they're having fun. Office papers are scattered all over the room. An air of the bully, almost a smell, comes off of Cucuzza's maintenance man's Tom: as Allan's Tom's Girl shouts the forbidden word "Daisy! Daisy! Daisy!" you can feel the punch coming before it lands on her face.

Tom's Girl, again an office worker, now with a bandage on her nose, is asleep on the couch. Nick is on the floor reading. More office workers come in. The place is a wreck; everyone cleans up for the big party at Gatsby's mansion. Nick is describing the party but the atmosphere is pure office. The crowd clears out. Nick is now quietly reading at his desk, as if pretending to work, the golfer is on the couch, and Jim, the all but invisible man at the other end of the desk, is speaking as Gatsby. He takes a call from Chicago and goes into the enclosure.

You struggle to connect any image of the character you might carry to this bland specter. "There was something gorgeous about him"—there's nothing gorgeous about him. His voice is unmodulated, self-protecting. He could be the head of the Fargo Chamber of Commerce worried about losing his job, as if a single high or low would crack his mask. With an eerie conviction, he captures the hollowness of Gatsby as he first begins to tell Nick who he is, that he is "the son of some wealthy people in the middle-west—all dead now," which is to say who he isn't, presenting himself in a way that Coleman Silk and Don Draper would have known wouldn't fool a child, as if as an actor Jim Fletcher has received the role in one piece from the zombie portrayals of Gatsby by Alan Ladd and Robert Redford. When Nick as a midwesterner himself asks, "'What part of the middle-west?'" and Jim answers "San Francisco," the lack of affect, the patent absence of reality—yes, San Francisco is in the middle of the West Coast of the United States, or anyway California, isn't that obvious?—is so strong you can think you're watching Gatsby with PTSD, either from losing Daisy or from what he saw and did in the war.

With the car crash at the end of the first of Gatsby's great parties that Nick attends, where he meets Gatsby for the first time, Nick is alone in the office as everyone else has gone out to look at the accident. "A sudden emptiness seemed to flow now from the windows and the great doors, endowing with complete isolation the figure of the host, who stood on the porch, his hand up in a formal gesture of farewell." The staging, placing these antitheatrical lines, which need the white silence of the page, in a theatrical setting so emptied it is like a blank page itself, brings out how luminous the lines are, how balanced, how full of portent and dread. It less dramatizes than pulls in, from a memory carried not only by the audience but by the characters who have yet to experience what they are now remembering, a fatal nostalgia: an anticipation that not only can anything vanish at any time, but, the feeling is as Shepherd reads, anything that does vanish may be too unmoored from its setting to be remembered at all. Here the spell is truly cast, as the bet the reading has made on giving each word its place begins to pay off. With ordinary theatrical or cinematic realism—locations, sets, costumes, makeup, hairstyles, every period detail correct—erased, realistic pacing, how people walk and talk, can also be erased, and as Shepherd reads, he can also pause, he can stop, to fill out an image in his mind just as you would do if you were reading. "It was one of those rare smiles with a quality of eternal reassurance in it, that you may come across four or five times in life," Shepherd reads as Nick tries to focus what made Gatsby different from anyone he'd ever met.

> It faced—or seemed to face—the whole external world for
> an instant, and then concentrated on *you* with an irresistible
> prejudice in your favor. It understood you just as far as you
> wanted to be understood, believed in you as you would like
> to believe in yourself, and assured you that it had precisely
> the impression of you that, at your best, you hoped to convey.

The rest of the paragraph, the rest of the encounter—"Precisely at that point it vanished—and I was looking at an elegant young rough-neck, a year or two over thirty, whose elaborate formality of

speech just missed being absurd"*—can be communicated by acting, with gestures and a dubious expression, an expression picking
up the way the bumping-into-itself repetition of *precisely* suggests
that the description of the man with the perfect smile is also a description of a con artist. But the disclaimer dissolves in the face of
the description as it first comes forth, because in the drama *Gatz*
makes, words finally trump all acts: what you see yields to what you
hear, to the way the play and its gestures let words echo as gestures
disappear.

Over Fletcher Henderson's hot "Can You Take It," Nick begins
to read out the names of all the people who went to Gatsby's parties
in the summer of 1922, with the supper before midnight and the
supper after, the orchestra playing the *Jazz History of the World*, the
swimming pool full of dandies and chorus girls whose names nobody knew. The story moves on—or, really, the story as the play lets
it out creates an atmosphere in which the words can breathe. *The
Great Gatsby*, Jim Fletcher said in 2012, "is kind of like what they
say about Afghanistan—nobody has ever successfully invaded it,
occupied it. So we didn't try to do that, we have all these revelations
because of seeing the actual book over and over again. But I think if
anybody tries to do an adaptation what they're trying to do is extract
something from it. What are they going to extract? The plot? The
storyline? The character? Daisy's character or Nick's character? Is

---

* As Chandler will say of Terry Lennox, the Gatsby in *The Long
Goodbye*, blink and the suave man of the world "could have stepped
right out of an old-fashioned kick-em-in-the-teeth gangster movie."

that where the essence of the book is?" When nothing is extracted, any phrase can glow.

As Lee Strasberg's Hyman Roth, standing in for the Jewish gangster Meyer Lansky, sitting Al Pacino's Michael Corleone down in his modest Florida house in the 1958 of *The Godfather, Part II*, a ballgame playing quietly in the background, says so bloodlessly, "I've loved baseball—ever since Arnold Rothstein fixed the World Series in 1919." Shepherd begins reading the part of the gambler Meyer Wolfsheim in an overdone Yiddish accent. But then Wolfsheim's part is taken over by Aaron Landsman's garage owner George, who sits down at the desk that's now the table in the elegant speakeasy where Jim Fletcher's Gatsby, Scott Shepherd's Nick, and Landsman's now corporeal Wolfsheim are having lunch and speaks without any accent at all—and in any context, the shock remains that Fitzgerald could so easily bring in a character who, as Gatsby tells Nick after Wolfsheim has left, "fixed the World's Series back in 1919."

It's an event that on the page, and on the stage as Fletcher says the line, as part of the fabric of the novel, has more weight than the fact of what, when the novel appeared, was not yet called the First World War. The war, as a part of history, something Nick and Gatsby and millions of other people took part in, makes sense. "To play with the faith of fifty million people," as Nick mulls the fact over, does not, and yet here he is, the man who pulled it off, sitting right across from Nick in a New York club filled with cops and bagmen, bootleggers and politicians, as real as Arnold Rothstein himself, who could have been sitting at the next table, chuckling as he overheard. Our collective memory of the First World War is vague and dim. Did Fitzgerald somehow sense that he was anchoring his story to an event that would never be forgotten, that the words "fixed the World's Series back in 1919" would, even for children born in the twenty-first century, instantly call up a violation as specific, as much or more a part of the American language, its inherent frame of reference, as the assassination of Abraham Lincoln, the Crash of 1929, or the attack on Pearl Harbor? "Arnold Rothstein bought the White Sox, including Shoeless Joe," says Damian Lewis's finance tycoon Bobby Axelrod in *Billions* in 2019. "Get it done."

As the golfer, sitting at the desk, remembers meeting Gatsby in 1917 in Louisville, when he and Daisy fell in love, she a celebrated debutante, he a lieutenant about to ship out, a transformation that has seemed an uncomplicated device for every other actor and character begins with *Gatz*'s Nick, who as the golfer is Jordan Baker and the maintenance man is Tom Buchanan has always stayed away from inhabiting Nick Carraway. Now, as in the shadows Tom's wife lies on the couch cradling a bottle, Susie Sokol's golfer is telling Nick about Daisy's marriage to Tom, how she found Daisy the day before the wedding drunk and with a letter from Gatsby in her hand, saying "Tell 'em all Daisy's change' her mine." The feeling in her voice is tense and scary, as if this is when the world, and the story, began to turn. Jordan is sitting next to Nick, who holds the book in his lap, his arm around Jordan, her head on his shoulder, and as they kiss he goes over into his character, and from this point on there will be an underlying tension to everything he does. He will always be Scott Shepherd, a reader thinking through what Nick Carraway has to say, and Nick Carraway, pulling away from Shepherd to say that this all really happened, that it's happening now.

The whole production is almost upended when Nick begins the scene where Gatsby and Daisy meet again, in Nick's own rented cottage, a plan cooked up by Daisy and Jordan, five years after the one-time lovers last saw each other, the five years when she didn't wait for her penniless soldier, sold him out and herself too by marrying a faithless swaggerer waving a string of pearls that by the time *Gatz* opened would have cost nearly four million dollars. The years when Gatsby came out of the war a hero, went back to Louisville to find Daisy gone but walked the streets as if he might find her hiding in the trees, then went to work with New York gangsters. The three years it took him to make the money, he will tell Nick, to buy a house too big to see all at once, even from the Buchanans' house across the bay, with the alluring green light at the end of its dock, which Gatsby so loved to gaze at in the night, from his own dock, knowing that someday he would draw those docks together and with Daisy in his arms he would reach for the light and twist it off, and with the drama he had lived finally complete, real life, real love, could begin. As Nick catches sight of the story before it really begins: "Fifty feet away a figure had emerged from the shadow of my neighbor's mansion and was standing with his hands in his pockets regarding the silver pepper of the stars. Something in his leisurely movements and the secure position of his feet upon the lawn suggested that it was Mr. Gatsby himself. . . . He stretched out his arms toward the dark water in a curious way, and, far as I was from him, I could have sworn he was trembling." Shepherd reads the words with such care that you can imagine Fitzgerald trembling as he wrote them.

To meet Daisy again, Jim comes back into the office in a white suit and white shoes. Gatsby is so nervous that in the novel, bare on the page, he makes the reader squirm, but here the scene runs as a kind of terrorized slapstick. It's Fatty Arbuckle on trial, as staged by the Keystone Kops. The scene is coming unmoored from itself, but soon enough the play breaks for an hour, and by the time the audience returns, knowing there are three hours to go, anticipation has to be its ruling passion.

The office is empty except for Lucille. Then Nick and the golfer sit at a desk together. Jim arrives in a pink jacket and red pants. Nick begins to read the story of Jimmy Gatz of North Dakota, as Gatsby told it to him on his last night, and again, as Jim sits like a statue, Nick brings out certain lines as fulcrums. "I suppose he'd had the name ready for a long time, even then. His parents were shiftless and unsuccessful farm people — his imagination had never really accepted them as his parents at all. The truth was that Jay Gatsby of West Egg, Long Island, sprang from his Platonic conception of himself." It was seventy-five years after *The Great Gatsby* appeared that Philip Roth published *The Human Stain*, where he fixed Gatsby's heroism and wove it, more directly, less subtly, and in a few stray, lightning moments as powerfully as Fitzgerald did, into the American fabric — as Fitzgerald shouted across the Atlantic the month before *The Great Gatsby* was published, under the red, white, and blue.

Roth tells the story of Coleman Silk, a seventy-one-year-old African-American from East Orange, New Jersey, who has passed as a Jew — as a white man — his entire adult life. As a professor and a dean of a small college in the Berkshires he has led a transformative life—he has transformed not only himself but his college and even the town around it—that calls to mind many others. In 2008, if one had happened to read the book then, it might have made you think of Barack Obama, not because he ever passed or ever could, but because as an African-American he seemed to have invented himself as absolutely as Coleman Silk. "What do we really know about this man?" John McCain asked throughout the fall campaign, and even without the innuendo—McCain rejected the accusations of his supporters that Obama was a Muslim, a communist, somehow even a terrorist, but purposefully or not he had planted them—the question hit home because it was about something real. Obama's very ease in his own skin—like Jackie Robinson in his ability to trust in his own gifts and never betray his rage at the slurs and lies that by election day at Republican rallies had become a torrent of hate, with crowds shouting "Kill him!" and "Traitor!" at the mention of his name—spoke for, Roth wrote of Coleman Silk, "the great frontier tradition, accepting the democratic invitation to throw your origins overboard if to do so contributes to the pursuit of happiness."

Obama, more like Gatsby than Coleman Silk—even if Silk and his lover die in a car crash that rewrites Daisy and Gatsby running over Myrtle Wilson—seemed like his own creation. That was the source of his aura, the sense of self-command that drew people to him, and it was at least partly the sense that he was not quite real, not quite human—as so indelibly with Gatsby that the moments when he does seem like a real person seem like miracles—that also terrified others, or repulsed them. As a kind of symbolic patriot, the self-invented American embodies America, a nation that was itself invented—"Every day," Roth wrote, "you woke up to be what you had made yourself"—but the self-invented American is also a kind of Frankenstein. As the story of the transformation of Jimmy Gatz into Jay Gatsby passes over the stage, Lucille tries to give Nick memos, but he keeps reading, his head bent down, until his head is resting on Jordan's knee. As the tale of Dan Cody, the millionaire miner who takes Jimmy Gatz around North America on his yacht as his spiritual son, rises up with Nick's voice, you get a clear view of how close the nearly lawless days of the gold and copper rushes really are in 1922, people appearing and disappearing and appearing again, Henry McCarty to Kid Antrim to William H. Bonney to Billy the Kid. "I remember the portrait of him up in Gatsby's bedroom," Nick reads, "a gray, florid man with a hard, empty face—the pioneer debauchee, who during one phase of American life brought back to the Eastern seaboard the savage violence of the frontier brothel and saloon." The words "one phase of American life" open up the story—they let you hear, in the contemplative spaces between the words as Shepherd reads them, how Fitzgerald was seeing, or trying to see, the whole arc of American history, keeping it in his mind's eye like a map tacked to the wall in front of his desk. Roth's purchase on the great frontier tradition to which he joined Coleman Silk may have come from the passage Nick is reading.

As Jim begins typing at his desk, there is Nick's warning to Gatsby not to demand from Daisy what she can't give, to say that she never loved Tom—"'I wouldn't ask too much of her,' I ventured. 'You can't repeat the past.' 'Can't repeat the past?' he cried incredulously. 'Why of course you can!'"—the famous lines sloughing off their fame as Shepherd turns them into speech, into something someone would actually say. The setting is quiet as Nick follows Daisy and Gatsby walking in Louisville five years before, when they met, allowing for an appearance of Jacob's Ladder so stunning as to take you out of the story to contemplate the poverty of your own imagination: "Out of the corner of his eye Gatsby saw that the blocks of the sidewalk really formed a ladder and mounted to a secret place above the trees—he could climb to it."

Shepherd's reading is so sure that it needs no inflection, no dramatization, for the passage that ends the chapter, as it could have ended the book, or almost any book: the words stand out in greater silence, and with greater weight, than perhaps they ever had on the page, where, really, you might be moving too fast, to find out what happens next, or to get again to the scenes that will blow everything apart. Gatsby is telling Nick the story, of a "tuning fork that had been struck upon a star. Then he kissed her"—you can hear the Crystals seal the words, as perhaps Fitzgerald's book gave them their song when in 1963 Phil Spector, Ellie Greenwich, and Jeff Barry batted phrases at each other as they wrote "Then He Kissed Me." "Through all he said," Shepherd reads, the line between him and Nick dissolved, meaningless, "even through his appalling sentimentality I was reminded of something—an elusive rhythm, a fragment of lost words, that I had heard somewhere a long time ago. For a moment a phrase began to take shape in my mouth and my lips parted like a dumb man's, as though there was more struggling on them than a wisp of startled air. But they made no sound, and what I had almost remembered was uncommunicable forever."

From this point on, it's the sound of the words that rule. You hear each word as if it could be lost—that feeling carried by the fact that the play is moving toward its end, where everything will be lost. In the forced confrontation where Nick, the golfer, Jim, Tom, and Tom's wife, Nick and Jordan and Gatsby and Tom and Daisy, are arrayed at Tom's house, Daisy's "voice struggled on through the heat, beating against it, molding its senselessness into forms"—it's a poor and meaningless sentence, except for the long fuse it lights, that "beating against," Fitzgerald casting a brief light on the image that will close the book, that Jennifer Love Hewitt moment, that "so we beat on, boats against the current." You can hear that, and you can hear that it's a Jennifer Love Hewitt moment because it's corny, a cliché as soon as it appears on the page in 1925, something that only takes away from the fact that before that line appears the book has already made its setting: "where the dark fields of the republic rolled on under the night." You can almost hear the cliché invading these words, too, as if they were just barely what they are not, what anyone else would have written, *rolled on through the night,* until Fitzgerald, and, it seems, Nick, step away from cliché, as the prairie rests before the gathering storm that the word "under" has brought into the image.

With the office now the Plaza Hotel in New York, the five sit in a dark room that regardless of the heat they all say they can't bear seems frigid as you watch. When with a power that is awful to take in Tom goes off on Mr. Nobody from Nowhere and the collapse of values and intermarriage between black and white, a recognizable American appears, a type and a person, and as Nick judges what's happening—"The transition from libertine to prig was so complete"—you realize how wrong George Will was when he watched the inauguration of Donald J. Trump as president of the United States and called him a Gatsby for our time. Adulterer or president, Trump was always Tom.

With Daisy driving Gatsby back from the Plaza Hotel, where Tom has driven a stake between her and Gatsby, after she had tried to tell Tom that she'd never loved him, that she's always loved Jay, and failing to convince Tom or even herself, after Tom has broken Gatsby down so far that he is not even again James Gatz, he is nothing, he has nowhere to go, with Cucuzza's Ralph Kramden Tom-voice enough to destroy Fletcher's awkward, stumbling Anybody, the office is convincingly a car. Myrtle Wilson's mechanic husband George convincingly carries a computer across the room as if it's a set of tools. The lights go up in the office, as Nick, riding in the office-car, reads as Daisy runs over Myrtle and keeps going. Lucille holds a memo for Nick. He goes to the desk. Tom checks the mail slots, as if looking for news.

Nick reads the passage where Gatsby goes back to Louisville after the war, then with Daisy gone boards the train north: "He stretched out his hand desperately as if to snatch only a wisp of air, to save a fragment of the spot she had made lovely for him. But it was all going by too fast now for his blurred eyes and he knew that he had lost that part of it, the freshest and the best, forever" — and in that overheated, overdone last sentence, as Shepherd reads it, again there is a fuse, another foreshadowing of a word that when it arrives will carry the force of everything that has come before it, all caught in the connection of "freshest" with, only a few more than twenty-five pages later, the "fresh, green breast of the new world." You don't make that connection as you read the book, but in the queer dramatic confusion here, as the ending that the audience knows from high school begins to exert a gravitational pull on every word that precedes it, the connection is the drama itself, the words pulling the story toward its end. But in truth the whole passage here is a fore-shadowing, a playing out of the drama that is present throughout, the "he stretched out his hand" falling like a stone into the last page of the book, when "his dream must have seemed so close that he could hardly fail to grasp it."

With Myrtle dead under Daisy's hand, Gatsby dead through Tom's fingering him by George's hand, George dead by his own — when, in the line that Fitzgerald could have had no idea what a wind history would put at its back, "the holocaust was complete" — with Tom and Daisy having packed up and disappeared, Nick is no longer reading. He holds the book, but he doesn't look at it. He has now gone over into Nick Carraway. Jim's corpse is laid out on the couch. Nick looks at it. He puts the book down. "When the but-ler brought back Wolfsheim's answer" — no, Wolfsheim can't really be at the funeral, he "'cannot get mixed up in this thing now'" — "I began to have a feeling of defiance, or scornful solidarity between Gatsby and me against them all" — and again that *against* pulls the words forward, to the ending now less than fifteen pages away, with the audience, feeling the presence of the ending, counting the pages down.

The few people willing to be there stand over the couch for Gatsby's funeral; then it's wheeled out. "The poor son-of-a-bitch" — Lucille is inside her cubicle, reading, not paying attention. Nick begins to make small, intimate gestures, bringing himself closer to the audience — the crowd in the theater, but also the world at large, the world that will, his tone and the slide of his shoulders say not with resignation but almost with satisfaction, take little notice of this story and forget it even if it does. He acts out the tale, on his way back to the West, "the real snow, our snow," speaking to the audience as he hasn't before, "unutterably aware of our identity with this country for one strange hour until we melted indistinguishably into it again." The snow plays the same role as the sea does with Tashtego as he nails the flag to the mast, and the patriotic air brings the audience into the identification Nick and Shepherd are both affirming and demanding. It's an identification that anyone listening, Nick and Shepherd are saying, must acknowledge for him or herself, so that the speaking of the words ties anyone listening into all the aspirations and lies of the story. It's Fitzgerald, but now it's a flesh-and-blood figure before you, carrying that physical authority, that bodily realism, binding Gatsby's story to the country's story, stating that they are identical.

As he speaks of the snow, of "our identity with this country," Shepherd's Nick is open, bright, with a huge weight pressing down on him that he shrugs off. In his posture, in his face — is he Nick, or is he Shepherd? In the audience you go back and forth, juggling the character and the actor, this reader as a stand-in for any other, not wanting any of them to hit the ground — he dares you to deny that he has taken the whole of this story into himself. The book is now resting on the desk in front of him. He begins to pull away from it. The momentum toward the end is unstoppable, but you can feel how deeply he is resisting the end, whatever it might be: no lesson, but an abandonment he can't countenance, let alone pass on. There is a weariness, not from the hours of performance, but of all the centuries piled up behind this small, trivial local crime story like a train, a story Vincent D'Onofrio's Bobby Goren would have wrapped up in sixty minutes, commercials included, though not without a look on his face that said the end of the show as set out in the script was too easy, wondering, as Nick at the end wonders if it wasn't Gatsby himself who had a hand in fixing the World Series, if it wasn't Gatsby who set up his own death, not Tom Buchanan, knowing when he left that hotel room that he was already dead.

Nick is alone in the room—so alone that any sense of history or time evaporates. Sitting behind the office table, facing the audience directly, he speaks now gesturing with his hands and arms in a way he hasn't done before. He smiles. There's now a palpable physical intimacy as he uses everything he has to get the story across, to absent himself from it, to let it unfold, and then fold back, on its own terms, in its own plain and exalted language. The final passages are recited, as if by a professor, or a preacher. It's a sermon, another errand into the wilderness.

In the wilderness, you don't know what you'll hear next, but you listen with a preternatural sharpness. Every broken twig increases the suspense. In Shepherd's pronunciation, back and forth between the syllables, "his dream must have seemed so close that he could hardly fail to grasp it," he finds a new and musical cadence. With the beat soft but unmistakable, you are pulled back to Gatsby leaving Louisville after the war, the listener in the audience not remembering so much as caught by "He stretched out his hand desperately as if to snatch only a wisp of air," and Shepherd realizes, and you realize, how fully the ground has been prepared, how trapped you are, how completely Fitzgerald has trapped Nick and Gatsby, by the words that dance through the story, by the gesture that plays the book like a piano. Shepherd reaches his hand out over the desk toward nothing, but then a deeper foreshadowing rises out of the spare, flat setting, the abandoned office matching Gatsby's abandoned house. "And as the moon rose higher the inessential houses melted away until gradually I became aware of the old island here that flowered once for Dutch sailors' eyes—a fresh, green breast of the new world," Nick says, as if he remembers this moment from three hundred years before on his own skin. As he goes on, to the end of the paragraph, where that first sighting slides into "face to face for the last time in history with something commensurate to his capacity for wonder," he physically reaches again, for the talisman, now shopworn with use, almost a Rosebud: "I thought of Gatsby's wonder when he first picked out the green light"—and you realize that, all along, that green light has signified not only Gatsby's story, but America itself.

That foreshadowing has been unfolding throughout the more than six hours Nick has been reading, listening to the words, listening to himself as he and others say them—foreshadowing is the eye of tragedy, and that, finally, as the new world itself becomes the green light the whole of the old world is sighting, is what rests on the stage. Nick opens the book and reads the last two paragraphs without much intonation, not needing what is now, after the weight and lightness of the gestures that have made up the play, their sentimental pleading, their flattery of the pure soul of both the writer and the reader. Scott Shepherd's Nick, Fitzgerald's Nick as Fitzgerald never imagined him, a different Nick, a reader who has both encountered the story and inherited it, maintaining the ragtime beat the words always contained, a quiet bang, bang, bang, bang. Sitting in the theater, I realized I was tapping my foot.

In a realm where art finds its familiars, it's the beat of "Mamie's Blues" as Jelly Roll Morton recorded it in New York, on December 16, 1939, less than two years before he died in Los Angeles at fifty, though he had likely been singing it in New Orleans brothels since the first years of the twentieth century. He was a pioneer of jazz—to hear him tell it, he invented it. In the twenties he set down such still-transporting numbers as "Wolverine Blues," "The Pearls," "Dead Man Blues," and "Mr. Jelly Roll." But in 1939 he was forgotten, a greeter and a piano player in a dive bar in segregated Washington, D.C. He had not made a commercial record in almost a decade.

For all the records he had made, he had never lighted down on "Mamie's Blues." It came out on the new General label, as a single 78 and as part of a five-disc 78 album called *New Orleans Memories*, which disappeared when the company folded in 1943, the recording then traveling to the present on countless LPs, CDs, YouTube uploads, with distortion or pristine but with the calmness of the performance always the first thing you heard. The song could be Gatsby's reply to Nick's attempt to understand what was so magical about Daisy's voice: "Her voice is full of money." Gatsby's tone as he speaks is described as awestruck in the novel, but the description is incomplete, hanging on the page, begging the question: that wasn't really all he meant, was it? That wasn't all he meant. Someone else has to answer that question. In the 1974 film, Redford delivers the line wistfully, looking up to heaven; in a scene shot but not used in Baz Luhrmann's movie, DiCaprio all but spits it out, bile in his throat. In *Gatz* Jim Fletcher delivers the line like a witness to a crime testifying against his will, which only raises more questions: what did she say, what did he hear, what does money mean, if it means anything but everything? As so many singers from Howlin' Wolf to Chuck Berry have defined the blues: "When you ain't got no *money*."

"Thank you for your letter," Fitzgerald wrote to a *Gatsby* fan in 1938, when he was as forgotten as Jelly Roll Morton, though he probably could have sung a few bars of "Wolverine Blues" if he had to. "It was very nice of you to go to all that trouble and it gave me a sense of 'Gatsby' still existing. I am sorry you didn't like Daisy's voice 'full of money.' I don't know whether 'a voice full of money' would charm me now, but I suppose I meant that it had a certain deep confidence that money gave in those days." But as Fitzgerald had written two years before, in 1936, of the success of *This Side of Paradise* and his marriage to Zelda Sayre, "It was one of those tragic loves doomed for lack of money, and one day the girl closed it out on the basis of common sense. During a long summer of despair I wrote a novel instead of letters, so it came out all right, but it came out all right for a different person. The man with the jingle of money in his pocket who married the girl a year later would always cherish an abiding distrust, an animosity, toward the leisure class—not the conviction of a revolutionist but the smouldering hatred of a peasant."

The tone of these words is like that of a suicide note from someone who has lost everything but his voice. The resentment, even a bare edge of sardonicism, is still alive on the table, but the body has been hanging from the beam for hours. The little reminiscence echoes back to that strange, seemingly thrown-away line on the second page of *The Great Gatsby*, "No—Gatsby turned out all right at the end," a line so odd it slips past its own narrative and into some literary ether. *He ended up doing the right thing in the end, so it doesn't matter that he also ended up shot to death in his own swimming pool?* A pool that, in a hint from a few pages later, a clue that too vanishes from the book, perhaps wasn't really Gatsby's pool at all, but merely part of the place that rented for twelve or fifteen thousand a season, not a stick of it Gatsby's, none of it more than a Wolfsheim Big Store.

"Mamie's Blues" fulfills the words Raymond Chandler came up with when describing *The Great Gatsby* in 1949: "somehow passing along, crystallized, complete, and as such things go nowadays eternal, a little pure art—great art or not I wouldn't know, but there is such a strange difference between the real stuff and a whole shelf full of Pulhams and Forsytes and Charlie Grays," which since seven decades later one likely has no idea who he's talking about would seem to make the point. "Mamie's Blues" too is complete in itself. As Ross Macdonald said of *The Great Gatsby*, the song opens doors in all directions, into the past and the future: "And they're still open; it hasn't been closed off at all." Kicking the tune around in Paris in the 1950s in his novel *Hopscotch*, Julio Cortázar's Argentine expatriates hear countless half-told stories in each phrase, intonation, hesitation, each wait before the dying fall of the last line of each verse.

As Morton played the song in 1939, there is a slow, opening theme on the piano, as if the keys depress from the pressure of fingers held above them. "This is the first blues I no doubt heard in my life," he says genially, but with the sense of a whole life lived behind him, and nothing he can touch ahead of him. "Mamie Desdunes," he says—"this is her favorite blues, she hardly could play anything else more, but she really could play this number. Of course to get in on it, to try to learn it, I made myself the, the can rusher"—the kid in the whorehouse who brings in beer from saloons.* He opens the song.

> 2:19 done took my baby away
> 2:19—took my babe away
> 2:17—bring her back someday

The lines embody the blues so fully they reach back to the stray, repeated sing-song mutterings of emancipated African-Americans free for the first time to wander the country, to ride its rails, to discover their own Americas. They embody the blues as a

---

* As part of a series of open, rambling sessions of interviews and performances recorded in Washington, D.C., by Alan Lomax in 1938, there is a very different version of the song, under the title "Buddy Bertrand's Blues." With the piano much more flamboyant and noisy, crowd-pleasing and in moments sentimental, with verses about back-door sex that are at once arty and guaranteed crowd pleasers, Morton gave a fuller introduction: "Here was among the first blues that I've ever heard, happened to be a woman, that lived next door to my god-mother's house in the Garden District. Her name was Mamie Desdunes. On her right hand, she had two middle fingers, between her forefingers, cut off, and she played with three. So she played a blues like this, all day long, when she would first get up in the morning."

social movement, and as a formal movement: as the record producer John Simon writes, while the first two lines of a protean blues
are the same, *"the chord underneath each of those sentences is different"* — and when "the chord under the second sentence changes,
it changes *one single note* in the melody — and that tiny change of
one note expresses all the pain, possibility, poignance that you now
can hear in every Blues Bar, from every Blues cover band in the
world." You hear that in "Mamie's Blues" as if it is a discovery that
has just been made, a magic lantern that has just appeared in Morton's hands. So he lets the rhythm, as if it is itself a train just beginning to pull out of the station, pull him forward:

> Stood on the corner with her feets, just soakin' wet (her feets
>   was wet)
> Stood on the corner with her feet, soaking wet
> Beggin' each and every man

— pressing down on *every man*, pushing the phrase a step or two
past the other words —

> that she met

— and then the drama, the action, right in a doorway, just barely
out of the rain, money changing hands, skirt hiked up, the lines
sung straight, as simple facts, nothing you can question, nothing
you can doubt —

> If you can't give me a dollar, give me a lousy dime
> Can't give me a dollar, give me a lousy dime
> I wanna feed, that hungry man of mine

Though Morton's introduction and the three verses take up all but the last thirty-five seconds of his two-minute, forty-some-second recording, in a way they're only the prelude to his real song. In a flurry of keys there's a sudden loud trill, as if he's starting a new theme. As he goes on, you wait for it to come up again, but it doesn't, and soon you know it won't. That was just to set you up for a long, slow slide. What comes through, now, as the piano continues to tease out a rolling count, is the softness of Morton's steadily tapping foot—and the softness is so distinct, so calls attention to itself, it's as if the sound is being made by a cushioned drum mallet on a carpet rather than a mere shoe.

It becomes the most subtle form of loudness. It draws you in. Morton plays contemplatively, letting you think, in his rhythm, about the immeasurable tiredness of everyday life, the casual rebukes and humiliations of ordinary commercial transactions, streetcars, shoes shined to make a good impression covered with the mud of a flooded street. He plays so slowly that silences begin to form in the cadence he's shaping, that's pulling him along, that he's following, and here that tapping foot is the only sign of unmediated human presence—of the fatalism that is half of blues—that you hear.

"She'd stepped on a rotten place and fallen through the floor and knew she was trapped in poverty forever," Ross Macdonald wrote in *The Goodbye Look* in 1969, in one of his many extensions of his favorite book: "The dream she was defending wasn't a dream for the future. It was a dreaming memory of the past, when she had lived in San Marino with a successful husband and a forty-foot pool." "'If you can't hand me a dollar, then hand me a rotten dime,'

Babs had said things like that in Cincinnati," Cortázar wrote, "every woman had said things like that somewhere, even in the bed of a king, Babs had a very special idea of what the bed of a king was like but in any case some woman must have said something like, 'If you can't give me a million, gimme a lousy grand.'" You can hear Daisy saying it, back in Chicago walking the Magnificent Mile sometime in the 1950s, or going from one room to another in her house in Beverly Hills in the 1960s, scattering hundred dollar bills behind her on the street or standing before the mirror in her bedroom fingering the pearl necklace she'd married for some forty years before, singing along with the Jelly Roll Morton LP spinning behind her in her room. Her voice was full of the memory of those times when money was really money; there wasn't a dime on her tongue.

THE FERMENT

Picture the 1920s as a drag race whose entries are ages vying for the Champion *gros-ben-age* of the times, that aura that remains after the flesh of the age has dropped away. The shimmering Etheric Double of the 1920s. The thing that gives it its summary. Candidates line up like chimeras.

—*Ishmael Reed*, Mumbo Jumbo, 1972

One underlying reason why *The Great Gatsby* has remained alive is that it absorbed the ferment of its time—"1920–1930. That 1 decade," as Ishmael Reed also puts it in *Mumbo Jumbo*, "which doesn't seem so much a part of American history as the hidden After-Hours of America struggling to jam. To get through." In 1925 Fitzgerald took into his book the action of the previous five years— the fortunes, crimes, and songs—and with such an acute sense of what the time wanted and what it feared that he was able to create an atmosphere in which the action of the next five years—the speculation, the panic, and the songs—had already taken place. The book set the decade to a rhythm that seemed both unnervably original and displacingly familiar when it was first heard, when it first appeared on the page, a rhythm no one has been able to resolve, that no one has been able to put to rest.

That is why the book is not merely read and taught almost a

hundred years after it was published, but why it has been continually taken up by other artists, its characters evolving into archetypes, or the characters brought down to earth and imbued with new personality in new work and then devolving back into archetypes that long precede the names Fitzgerald gave them. It's why the book works as both a grounding and a locus point for anyone's consideration of the American subject—the deadly dance between America's promises and their betrayal. A certain nihilist impulse emerged from an incomprehensible war into a cornucopia of money—a war that, many felt even at the time, less settled any peace than set the stage for the next war, and cut the boards out from under any platform from which leaders would presume to order affairs. That nihilist strain, not unrelated to the fact that because of Prohibition a good part of the citizenry was as a matter of everyday life breaking the law, drove countless people to experiment, to do what had never been done and say what had never been said, whether in art or in life. You could say almost anything and get away with it. Ma Rainey's 1928 "Prove It On Me Blues," made with the Tub Jug Washboard Band, lurching from beat to beat with a bottle in one hand and a silver Derringer in the other, a lesbian anthem in the form of a hangover—"Went out last night with a crowd of my friends / They must have been women, 'cause I don't like no men"—wasn't scandalous, it was a shrug. The song was a miniature of one of Gatsby's parties as they're staged in Baz Luhrmann's movie: you can see it sung on the stage set up over the swimming pool, and you can imagine Ma Rainey showing up with all her girlfriends. There was a faith that anything was possible and that nothing one did was of any consequence at all, which meant, in words that could have found their way into Hoagy Carmichael's 1927 "Washboard Blues" without a stitch in the beat, that there was no success like failure and that failure was no success at all.

The era *The Great Gatsby* wrote was a bacchanal that left every question worth asking hanging in the air. "What form do you suppose a life would take," Walter Benjamin asked at the end of the decade, "that was determined at a decisive moment by the street song last on everyone's lips?" That song—the song the time sang, the song that sang the time—contained an allure that, too, is still hanging in the air. Every so often the ear of a time that came after tips back to catch the tune.

The tune—the culture—retains its power because in the 1920s government—the official site of authority in American life—had all but quit the field. That meant the field was open. Under the Republican administrations of Harding, Coolidge, and Hoover, the federal government abdicated any responsibility for what the Constitution called the general welfare. It functioned mainly punitively: to break strikes, block unions, jail and deport accused subversives, and keep people poor. As the decade accelerated, the wealth of one percent of the population exceeded that of the lowest ninety percent—the most grievous establishment of income inequality, of the dictatorship of money, in American history since the introduction of the income tax in 1913, at least as I write. As an arbiter in national life, government was replaced by fly-by-night businesses that whether they were automobile companies or radio churches were across the decade felt as both illusions and institutions. The real governments of the 1920s were organized crime, a new Ku Klux Klan in both the North and the South, the stock market, and jazz.

These governments made crossing arguments about form and ontology. Fitzgerald, somewhat slickly, composing a backdated fanfare, in a 1937 piece for *Esquire*:

> America was going on the greatest, gaudiest spree in history and there was going to be plenty to tell about it. The whole golden boom was in the air—its splendid generosities, its outrageous corruptions and the tortuous death struggle of the old America in prohibition. All the stories that came into my head had a touch of disaster in them—the lovely young creatures in my novels went to ruin, the diamond mountains of my short stories blew up, my millionaires were as beautiful and damned as Thomas Hardy's peasants. In life these things hadn't happened yet, but I was pretty sure living wasn't the reckless, careless business these people thought—this generation just younger than me.

And again in Ishmael Reed's words, a drag race:

> The Age of Harding pulls up, the strict upper-lip chrome. The somber, swallow-tailed body, the formal top-hatted hood, the overall stay-put exterior but inside the tell-tale poker cards, the expensive bootlegged bottle of liquor, and in the back seat the whiff of scandal. The Age of Prohibition: Speaks, cabarets, a hearse with the rear-window curtains drawn over its illegal contents destined perhaps for a funeral at sea.
>
> Now imagine this Age Race occurring before a crowd of

society idlers you would find at 1 of those blue-ribbon dog shows. The owners inspecting their pekinese, collies, bull-dogs, german shepherds, and then observe these indignant spectators as a hound mongrel of a struggle-buggy pulls up and with no prior warning outdistances its opponents with its blare of the trumpet, its crooning saxophone, its wild inelegant Grizzly Bear steps.

"It would take a few months," Reed goes on, taking a story from Irene Castle's memoir *Castles in the Air*, "before a woman would be arrested for walking down a New Jersey street singing 'Everybody's Doing It Now.'"

In 1939 Fitzgerald was in Hollywood, broke, a joke, a failed screenwriter all but blacklisted by the studios as a ruined alcoholic, trying desperately to find any movie work he could and not drink. As an old Ivy League party boy he was teamed with the young screenwriter Budd Schulberg to revisit, at the one remove of Dartmouth, Schulberg's alma mater, his own glory days at Princeton, to retrace the spiritual steps of his first and, at the time, his only remembered novel, the 1920 runaway best seller *This Side of Paradise*, where privileged young men do irresponsible things with wide, sad grins ("Not real Fitzgerald," Ross Macdonald said in 1972, stating the obvious that most who celebrate Fitzgerald ignore, "by the standard that he later set"). The two were to go to the iconic Dartmouth Winter Carnival and then write a winter carnival movie. Away from the ordered, predictable, accountable Hollywood routines he had so carefully cultivated, Fitzgerald drank himself into dementia and was fired; *Winter Carnival* came out with writers' credit to Schulberg, Lester Cole, and Maurice Rapf.* In 1950, Schulberg, by then famous for his scabrous 1941 Hollywood satire *What Makes Sammy Run?* published *The Disenchanted*, a novel about the Dartmouth trip. It was a hit, and helped start the conversation Fitzgerald and the country have been engaged in ever since.

The conversation takes its first form when the washed-up bore Manley Halliday, the purposely transparent Fitzgerald character, is trying to tell Schulberg's young left-wing Shep Stearns why Stearns was born too late.† Though the voice, pushed by Schulberg's Wil-

---

* "I won't forget the real pleasure of knowing you," Fitzgerald wrote Schulberg afterward, along with suggestions on how to make certain *Winter Carnival* scenes work, "and your patience as I got more and more out of hand under the strain. In retrospect, going East under those circumstances seems one of the silliest mistakes I ever made."

† In 1955 Schulberg won an Oscar for his screenplay for *On the Waterfront*—a film about a longshoreman's struggle over whether to testify against the mob bosses who control his union; Elia Kazan also won for direction. In 1951 Schulberg, and in 1952 Kazan, as former members of the Communist Party, appeared before the House Committee on Un-American Activities and named their former comrades and others in their orbit. Many of those they exposed had their careers and their lives destroyed. (*Winter Carnival* co-writers Maurice Rapf and Lester Cole were both Communists and both blacklisted in 1947; Cole was a member of the Hollywood Ten and served ten months in prison for refusing to testify before Congress. In 1978, according to his autobiography, *Hollywood Red*, he called in to a radio show where Schulberg was the guest: "Aren't you the canary who sang before the un-American Committee?" Cole relates saying. "Just sing,

shire Boulevard cockiness, has a crude pathetic overtone and none
of Fitzgerald's delicacy, it can serve for the claim Fitzgerald probably made for his time, with little held back. Lay it over Nick Carraway's rundown of the people who came to Gatsby's parties, and you
have Fitzgerald's spree:

> Our age forced moral decisions on us that seem to me to
> make for better art. In this decade of yours, a playwright like
> Odets yells STRIKE and everybody puts him up with Chekov
> and Ibsen. You can talk about your Depression Renaissance,
> these Writers and Artists Projects and all the rest. But just
> think of what we had: *The Waste Land* and Pound and Cum-
> mings—your poets are midgets compared to them—and our
> novelists. Why, in one year, 1925, we published *An Ameri-
> can Tragedy, Arrowsmith,* Dos Passos' *Manhattan Transfer,*
> and *The Great Gatsby.* And books by Ellen Glasgow, Willa

canary, sing, you bastard!") In 1999, when Kazan received an honorary
Oscar, some still heard him speaking in 1952. Steven Spielberg did not
rise, and Amy Madigan, Ed Harris, and Nick Nolte stayed in their seats
and did not applaud. There is no telling what Fitzgerald might have
done. "It is not that you should not disagree with them—the important
thing is that you should not argue with them," he wrote of Communists
in 1940 to his daughter. "The point is that Communism has become an
intensely dogmatic and almost mystical religion and whatever you say
they have ways of twisting it into shapes which put you in some lower
category of mankind ('Fascist,' 'Liberal,' 'Trotskyist') and disparage you
both intellectually and personally in the process. They are amazingly
well organized."

Cather, Tom Boyd, Edith Wharton, Elinor Wylie and some
I've forgotten. Yes, and our stage was alive. We had O'Neill
of course, and the Theater Guild really stood for something
and there were intelligent plays by George Kelly, Max Anderson and Elmer Rice, Don Stewart—Eddie Mayer. And we
had actresses, Cornell and Helen Hayes, Judith Anderson and
Laurette Taylor, and Pauline Lord, Jane Cowl and Ina Claire.
Oh, sure, they're still around but believe me, they aren't the
same. We were all in love with our stars—maybe that made
the difference. There was something special about those days.
People were wittier and they did things better. And we knew
how to give them that feeling that they were better than anyone had ever been before. . . . And the songs, why were our
songs so much better, *Embraceable You* and *My Man* and
Who—I'll never forget the first time I heard Marilyn Miller
sing it—and the Garrick Gaieties, *Now tell me what street
compares with Mott Street in July* . . . you don't have anyone
who twinkled like Marilyn Miller, haunted you like Jeanne
Eagles—I even think our movie stars were better, Valentino
was so much more what he was than any of yours today, and
Doug had more energy and Pickford and Gish were more
wistful, Barbara La Marr and Swanson were more stunning
and Carmel Meyers was wickeder and Colleen Moore was
cuter and Alyce Joyce and Billie Dove had that breath-taking
beauty you don't see anymore. And we had Lindy. God how
we loved Lindy. Maybe that's what's gone—that capacity for
abstract love. Anyway, it seems rather symbolic, doesn't it,

your Charles A. Lindbergh, the appeaser and our Lindy, the blue-eyed boy, the Lone Eagle, Horatio Alger in an airship conquering space.*

And there was so much more that just to say the names of those who first appeared or came into their own in the twenties — were brought into their own by the time itself — is as thrilling as it is humbling. Louis Armstrong. Faulkner. Hemingway. Dashiell Hammett. Bix Beiderbecke. Erich von Stroheim and *Greed*, Al Jolson and *The Jazz Singer*. Sophie Tucker, Laurel and Hardy, and Buster Keaton. The emergence of southern singers capturing another, fatalistic, free-swinging America in music that had been taking shape for a generation before it began to appear on 78s in 1926 and took the form of art: Blind Lemon Jefferson, Charlie Poole, the Carter Family, Jimmie Rodgers, Dock Boggs, Tommy Johnson, Frank Hutchison, Charley Patton, Son House, Clarence Ashley, the Memphis Jug Band, the Reverend J. M. Gates. Bessie Smith. The reinvention of photography by Berenice Abbott, Dorothea Lange, Paul Strand, Clarence White, Margaret Bourke-White, Ansel Adams,

---

* "It was painful and disorienting: Halliday standing up for *his* heroes — *his* beauties — *his* songs," Schulberg's Stearns character thinks after Halliday finishes. "For here was tacit acceptance of the morbid arithmetic that he had ceased to live beyond 1929. Actually, Halliday had been — was still — a young man in the Thirties. Yet he seemed to see nothing strange in regarding the Thirties as an age in which he was only an interloper, if not a phantom, a man who spoke of himself as ten years dead."

and Man Ray. The upheavals of the Logan County War in West Virginia, the trial and executions of Sacco and Vanzetti in Massachusetts and the Tom Mooney trial in Chicago. Berlin and Gershwin, Houdini and Josephine Baker, Mickey Mouse and Frank Lloyd Wright. James Weldon Johnson, Jean Toomer, Claude McKay, Zora Neale Hurston, Countee Cullen, and Langston Hughes's *The Weary Blues.* Thomas Hart Benton and Georgia O'Keeffe. Edna St. Vincent Millay, Anita Loos, Ethel Waters, and the 1923 Jordan Playboy—not the car, not many saw that, but the ad, which everybody saw, and which probably named Jordan Baker. Beneath a drawing that communicates quickness more than anything else, with a figure on a galloping horse just behind a flapper at the wheel of a top-down roadster, there's this text, in a literary typeface:

> Somewhere west of Laramie there's a broncho-busting, steer-roping girl who knows what I'm talking about.
>
> She can tell what a sassy pony, that's a cross between greased lightning and the place where it hits, can do with eleven hundred pounds of steel and action when he's going high, wide and handsome.
>
> The truth is—the Playboy was built for her.
>
> Built for the lass whose face is brown with the sun when the day is done of revel and romp and race.
>
> She loves the cross of the wild and the tame.
>
> There's a savor of links about that car—of laughter and lilt and light—a hint of old loves—and saddle and quirt. It's a brawny thing—yet a graceful thing for the sweep o' the Avenue.

Step into the Playboy when the hour grows dull with
things gone dead and stale.

Then start for the land of real living with the spirit of
the lass who rides, lean and rangy, into the red horizon of a
Wyoming twilight.

"An eagerness and a zest: they have elbow room here for their
racing; they can drive on as far as they like; they have an unknown
country to explore, a country that no one has ever heard of"—
Edmund Wilson might have thought he was writing prophecy in
1922 in his "Night Thoughts in Paris"; he was really writing copy for
the Jordan Playboy.

Other than a single note in Louis Armstrong's "Gut Bucket
Blues," little captures this cultural waterfall with more verve and
ambition than Fitzgerald's friend Gilbert Seldes's *The 7 Lively Arts*,
an affirmation of movies, radio, newspaper satire, comic strips, the
Broadway revue, jazz, Hollywood comedy, and far more, written
in Paris, from memory, out of a kind of nostalgia for the present:
1924, right at the center of all that had already happened and everything that was to come. It's still stirring to read because no one has
ever answered Edmund Wilson's bedrock charge more directly. As
if asked, as Wilson asked, for what drama his setting was the setting,
Seldes replied two years later as if he'd spent that time weighing
an answer. "It is a pleasure to come upon an accredited master-
piece which preserves its authority, to mount the stairs and see the
Winged Victory and *know* that it is good," he wrote in "Before a
Picture by Picasso," the last chapter in the book—on *The Lovers*,
which he'd just seen in Picasso's studio. "But to have the same con-

viction about something finished a month ago, contemporaneous in every aspect, yet associated with the great traditions of painting, with the indescribable thing we think of as the high seriousness of art and with a relevance not only to our life, but to life itself—that is a different thing entirely."

Most of the great works of art have reference to our time only indirectly—as they and we are related to eternity. And we require arts which specifically refer to our moment, which create the image of our lives. There are some twenty workers in literature, music, painting, sculpture, architecture, and the dance who are doing this for us now—and doing it in such a manner as to associate our modern existence with that extraordinary march of mankind which we like to call the progress of humanity. It is not enough. In addition to them— in addition, not in place of them—we must have arts which, we feel, are for ourselves alone which no one before us could have cared for so much, which no one after us will wholly understand. The picture by Picasso could have been admired by an unprejudiced critic a thousand years ago, and will be a thousand years hence. We require, for nourishment, some- thing fresh and transient. It is this that makes jazz so much the characteristic art of our time and Jolson a more typical figure than Chaplin, who is also outside of time.

That is Seldes's affirmation not only of his time, but of any time. It's a portable manifesto. It can go anywhere. That's why his book is still read, and why it still forms the values of people who have never heard of it. And yet it's impossible to imagine a similar book from the 1910s or the 1930s traveling so well. Either because of the edge of Seldes's taste or the way the people he wrote about were at once authors and audiences of their time, it can bring you up short when you realize how many of the people he celebrated are still part of the American conversation.

Seldes was part of Fitzgerald's literary conversation. Fitzgerald was consumed by the need to see the review of *The Great Gatsby* Seldes promised he was writing. "If you get a proof of your *Dial* review please send it to me as I can't wait to see the magazine — having only three even decent reviews. Burton Rascoe says *The Great Gatsby* is just Robert Chambers with overtones of *Nedra* by Harald Nigrath. So I think I'll write a 'serious' novel about the Great Struggle the Great American Peasant has with the Soil. Everyone else seems to be doing it. Burton will be the hero as I'm going to try to go to 'life' for my material from now on." He couldn't have been disappointed. "Fitzgerald has ceased to content himself with a satiric report on the outside of American life and has with considerable irony attacked the spirit underneath, and so has begun to report on life in its most general terms," Seldes wrote in the number for August 1925. "His tactile apprehension remains so fine that his people and his settings are specifically of Long Island; but now he meditates upon their fate, and they become universal also."

What makes Seldes's book of a piece with his subjects is that by writing with love, passion, noisiness, and a capacity always to be surprised, he puts the shock over how deep and how high culture can go — the everyday culture of everyday life — on the page. Quoting Clive Bell, a critic from the Bloomsbury milieu —

> The encouragement given to fatuous ignorance to swell
> with admiration of its own incompetence is perhaps what
> has turned most violently so many intelligent and sensitive
> people against Jazz. They see that it encourages thousands of
> the stupid and the vulgar to fancy that they can understand

art, and hundreds of the conceited to imagine that they can create it

— Seldes finds his antimanifesto: *My God, people might actually know why they like what they like! Where might that lead? Why, next they'll throw everything overboard and have intermarriage between black and white!* "The lively arts have never had criticism," Seldes writes in a final counter. "But the lively arts can bear the same continuous criticism which we give to the major, and if the criticism itself isn't bogus there is no reason why these arts should become self-conscious in any pejorative sense." He trusts what he loves, and strikes back against people who think he's putting on a literary vaudeville act—that after the show is over he'll go home and wipe off the greasepaint, or the blackface. "It is claimed," he says, that he and his like, critics who pretend to criticize what isn't worth the word, ". . . *cannot* care for the lively arts, unless they romanticize them and find things in them which aren't there." Seldes died in 1970; perhaps he was lucky enough to come across the November 3, 1968, issue of *Rolling Stone*, with Jonathan Cott's interview with John Lennon. "Pop analysts are often trying to read something into songs that isn't there," Cott said. "It is there," Lennon came right back. "It's like abstract art really. It's just the same really."

While always in tune with the largest questions—what culture is, what it's for, where it comes from, how it seizes novelty and fights off cliché, how it creates meaning and loses it—Seldes wrote with the refusal to apologize or make excuses that was the quality that most drew him to his subjects. That is present less in his hobbled oracular pronouncements—of Keystone comedy: "It shook us because it was really the earth trembling beneath our feet"; of Chaplin: "He stood then shod in absurdity, but with his feet on the earth"—than when he tries to get at why a Ziegfeld Follies revue can be life itself. He starts with the division between high art and low art, and, as if remembering what to Melville was the obvious fact that the American "is bound to carry republican progressiveness into Literature," with the interesting, antidemocratic fact that higher standards seem always to be applied to the low than the high.

> In producing serious plays, in writing great novels, we will stand for a second-rateness we would not for a moment abide in the construction of a bridge or the making of an omelette, or the production of a revue. And because in a revue the bunk doesn't carry

—and that is a line to carry around—

> the revue is one of the few places you can go with the assurance that the thing, however tawdry in itself, will be well done. If it is tawdry, it is so in keeping with the taste of its patrons, and without pretense; whereas in the major arts—no matter how magnificent the masquerade of Art may be—the taste of a production is usually several notches below the taste of the patrons.

With an ardor that makes you want to see and hear what he does, Seldes dives into an act made for a Gatsby party, precisely a *Jazz History of the World*:

> At the Follies passes Gilda Grey, a performer of limited talents gifted with unutterable intensity. Against a flaring back-

ground in which all the signs of all of Broadway are crowded together, she sings a commentary on the negro invasion—*It's Getting Very Dark on Old Broadway*—the scene fades and radiolite picks out the white dresses of the chorus, the hands and faces recede into undistinguishable black. And while the chorus sings Miss Grey's voice rises in a deep and shuddering ecstasy to cry out the two words, "Getting darker!"

If you can't see that now, you can see Gray in a set piece that could have come from the same show: a fifteen-minute 1931 Frankie and Johnny short called *He Was Her Man*. In a saloon, Gray's Frankie dances while Nellie Bly, seated at a table, catches the eye of Walter Fenner's much lower-billed sleazeball Johnny and pulls her skirt up her leg. As they go off together, black janitors rotate Gray's reflection in gleaming spittoons, and the film breaks out into a sweeping multiple exposure as Gray swings back and forth. When the band slides the music into "Frankie and Johnny," Gray seems to make a statement: whatever Nellie Bly and Frankie are doing in the back room, it can't be half as good as what she has in mind. In the way she tilts her body to one side as she cocks her head to the other, without a word she steals the Jolson trademark: *You ain't seen nothin' yet!* She offers herself to a pagan god: the God of Shimmy, and so outrageously you have to watch her over and over again to make sure you really saw what you saw—or how, even before the enforcement of the Hays Code in Hollywood, it got past the censors.

Then Frankie goes and buys a gun from a Jewish pawnbroker.

The lively arts, Seldes writes, "are almost secret to us, like the mysteries of a cult," and he is willing to talk that talk. In the likes of Gilda Gray, "a wholly unrealistic, imaginative presentation of the way we think and feel is accomplished." But he wants to go farther. "One man on the American stage, and one woman, are possessed—Al Jolson and Fanny Brice," he writes in a chapter titled "The Daemonic in the American Theatre." He means what Ishmael Reed means in *Mumbo Jumbo*, the chronicle of Jes Grew, a dance craze spreading from the South to the Midwest to New York, where it will either conquer the world, sweeping aside all structures of power, or die: "This," says a doctor in a triage ward in New Orleans, "is a *psychic epidemic*, not a lesser germ like typhoid fever or syphilis. We can handle those. This belongs under some ancient Demonic Theory of Disease." Jolson and Brice, Seldes says, two Jewish singers, dancers, and comedians, are "all we have of the Great God Pan, and we ought to be grateful for it. For in addition to being more or less a Christian country, America is a Protestant community and a business organization—and none of these units is peculiarly prolific in the creation of daemonic individuals." He's writing with blinders—Seldes's own *The Stammering Century*, from 1928, followed a vast parade of white Antinomian heretic–Protestant perfectionist cult leaders marching through the 1800s into his own time—but Seldes is looking for what happens outside of that Protestant community, where people speak the language of break on through, which is as true a native tongue as lock the door.

He means the way Jolson holds nothing back, and the unrestricted gaiety Brice can conjure up with gestures ("the magic must reside in her incredible elbow"), asides, shifts in tone so light they can be felt but never pinned down. And he means that these two people are not only, and sometimes not at all, exactly themselves:

they are vehicles for desires their audiences cannot express and fears they cannot even admit. On certain nights, "Jolson is driven by a power beyond himself. One sees that he knows what he is doing, but one sees he doesn't half realize the power and intensity with which he is doing it." Brice, without any display of force or even intent, demolishes every trace of convention and restraint. With the white elephants of genteel culture, Seldes says, "she always creates the original in the very process of destroying it." Even before she gets to burlesque she "has fatally destroyed the whole tedious business of polite and sentimental concert-room vocalism." And it is because they are Jewish, "racially out of the dominant caste," that they can burrow from within, until perhaps the whole edifice of polite culture collapses on itself. "The medium in which they work requires more decency and less frankness than usually exist in our private lives," Seldes says, "but within these bounds Jolson and Brice go farther, go with more contempt for artificial notions of propriety, than anyone else."

But finally Seldes's conventionally critical language fails to rise to his ideas, or simply what he wants, and he has to veer toward the voice of a novelist. To say what this art is, what it's for, what the country wants, what *it* is for, to enshrine the art that everyone deserves, the art that allows those who are willing to be changed by it to say this is for ourselves alone, something no one before us could have cared for so much, and which no one after us will wholly understand—though again, like so many of the people Seldes took up in *The 7 Lively Arts*, Jolson and Brice, like Irving Berlin, Chaplin, or George Herriman, are still with us, as presences or signposts—Seldes has to place his bet on metaphor. He has to write like Fitzgerald, to find the voice Nick Carraway would have reached for in those moments when he tried to make sense of how the little private drama that entangled him was at once the whole of the American prospect and the whole American curse. "I use the word possessed," Seldes wrote, "because it connotes a quality lacking elsewhere on the stage, and to be found only at moments in other aspects of American life — in religious mania, in good jazz bands, in a rare outbreak of mob violence. . . . You may see it on the Stock Exchange, and you can see it, canalized and disciplined, but still intense, in our skyscraper architecture."

He keeps coming back to that word *intense* — that is the special quality of the age he wants to fix. And he does, even though he was writing a very self-limiting book. Outside of Chaplin and Mack Sennett, here American culture exists only in Manhattan. The book is prima facie addressed specifically and only to white readers: "The negro is more intense than we are," he says. He goes on as if he were Tom Buchanan, if Buchanan were a literary critic, not a polo player: "I say the negro is not our salvation because with all my feeling for what he instinctively offers, for his desirable indifference to our set of conventions about emotional decency, I am on the side of civilization." "More must be said of the negro side of jazz," Seldes says — you wince: the Negro *side?* — "than I can say here," and in a nearly 400-page book, across a page and a half he addresses himself to precisely three black artists (he didn't know that George Herriman, who to Seldes had only Chaplin as his "one compeer" among American artists, was African-American): the ragtime composers Noble Sissle and Eubie Blake, and the blues composer and bandleader W. C. Handy, each mentioned, and indexed, only by last name. Irving Berlin is the king of ragtime and Paul Whiteman is the king of jazz.* Armstrong and Beiderbecke don't exist; neither do Mamie Smith with her "Crazy Blues" opening up a national audience of black and white in 1920 or Bessie Smith with her "Tain't Nobody's Biz-ness If I Do" three years after that. There is no register of any stirring of the Harlem Renaissance, of which *Mumbo Jumbo* is, in its hoodoo-detective-story way, a version—and yet it was out of the Harlem Renaissance that came, after Seldes wrote but altogether of its time and the spirit of the time he was trying to catch, the perfect manifesto of the artistic intensity, the ambition, the drive, and the demonic he was after.

The one-issue 1926 Harlem literary magazine *FIRE!!* affirmed the ferment that fed the energies of the decade into Fitzgerald's book—energies that would keep the story it told unsatisfied, with both the story itself and those who heard it wanting so hard for it to come out differently—and as a magazine *FIRE!!* seemed to want in the same moment to make history and let history burn it up. It wasn't afraid to sound pretentious, absurd, even adolescent if that's what it took. The manifesto carried the name "Foreword," which the words that followed burned off in an instant.

> *FIRE . . . flaming, burning, searing and penetrating far beneath the superficial items of the flesh to boil the sluggish blood.*

---

* Seldes does allow that had the black bandleader Jim Europe lived beyond 1919, he would have been greater than Whiteman.

FIRE . . . a cry of conquest in the night, warning those who sleep and revitalizing those who linger in the quiet places dozing.

FIRE . . . melting steel and iron bars, poking livid tongues between stone apertures and burning wooden opposition with a cackling chuckle of contempt.

FIRE . . . weaving vivid, hot designs upon an ebon bordered loom and satisfying pagan thirst for beauty unadorned . . . the flesh is sweet and real . . . the soul an inward flush of fire . . . Beauty? . . . flesh on fire—on fire in the furnace of life blazing . . .

"Fy-ah,
Fy-ah, Lawd
Fy-ah gonna burn ma soul!"

"Poetry is either something that lives like fire inside you—like music to the musician or Marxism to the Communist—or else it is nothing," Fitzgerald wrote to his daughter in 1940, fourteen years after the building housing the *FIRE!!* office burned down. That was the spirit of the twenties, and quietly, slowly, with that ragtime beat, that was the spirit Fitzgerald meant for "the man who gives his name to" the book he published on the heels of Seldes's snapshot of 1924.

AT THE MOVIES

After his death a friend of Wendy's told me that his great talent had been to make other people—friends, loved ones, other actors—better by getting them to risk more. He played characters who fucked up and took their lumps as a result. Either that or they got sucker punched by circumstance and had to take a standing eight count. As their losses mounted, their inner flame would gutter, and you'd wonder if they'd throw in the towel, because in their place that's what you'd do. But it always remained, that flickering flame, waiting to be fanned. That was Wendy's temperament, his films were invariably about his characters' attempts to relocate the shed skin of a better self, about somehow slipping back into it, feeling at home in it once more.

By contrast, Nolan was the reliable, competent American Everyman, the Nick Carraway who would never understand or accept or like himself half as much as Gatsby did.

—*Richard Russo, "Milton and Marcus," in* Trajectory, 2017, *on his characters Wendell "Wendy" Percy, based on his encounters with Paul Newman, and William Nolan, based on his encounters with Robert Redford.*

"Clark Gable wants to do it but Paramount is playing dog-in-the-manger about the rights," Fitzgerald wrote to a *Gatsby* fan in 1938. "Griffith"—Edward H. Griffith, the director of *Honeymoon in Bali,* on which Fitzgerald worked uncredited—"has always wanted to do 'The Great Gatsby' over again as a talkie," Fitzgerald wrote to a Hollywood agent a year later. In the 1940s Raymond Chandler thought he had a chance at it, but option conflicts sidelined the project. It wasn't until 1949 that Paramount went ahead with a picture starring Alan Ladd as Gatsby and as Daisy Betty Field, a stage actress with the features of a 1950s sitcom best friend who couldn't hold a movie screen. Based on the 1926 theatrical adaptation, or compression, by Owen Davis, and directed and acted without highs or lows, it's notable mostly because Howard Da Silva, who played George Wilson, would turn up in the 1974 Robert Redford remake as Meyer Wolfsheim; because the original director of the Ladd production, John Farrow, who quit when he wasn't allowed to cast Gene Tierney as Daisy, was the father of Mia Farrow, who would play Daisy to Redford's Gatsby; and because the picture was one of the most enervating movies ever made, from first to last a suffocating exercise in moralism.* In the opening scene, Macdonald Carey's Nick, who has a businessman's moustache and oddly towers over everyone else on the screen, and his wife, Jordan Baker, the relentlessly unglamorous Ruth Hussey, who's so properly dressed she's hard to see, arrive at Gatsby's grave twenty years after the 1928 in which the film is set, presumably to make it seem less far away and more marketable than the novel's 1922. They're there to muse over their flaming youth ("He

---

* The writers had clearly terrorized themselves over fear of the Hays office: Gatsby and Daisy's love, which threatens a marriage, could be papered over, and anyway he dies, but Tom and Myrtle's couldn't, even if *she* dies, so Tom has to become a moral figure: not only does he not rat out Gatsby to Wilson, he desperately tries to call Gatsby to tell him Wilson is gunning for him, and when he can't get through, calls the police to warn *them*. That allows for dramatic sirens on the soundtrack as soon as the shots are fired.

seems like someone we knew in another time, another life, another world," Jordan says. "Jazz, prohibition, flaming youth") and gaze at the tombstone. "It's not his style," Jordan says of the simple pillar. "No," says Nick, "he'd have fancied something more like Grant's Tomb. . . . Big dream, big drive. I liked him for what he might have been," he says, whatever that might mean, beyond establishing the condescension of the living toward the dead. The setting is bathed in bland light. Movements are stiff. The sky is bored. Jordan asks about the inscription: PROVERBS 14.12. "Did you arrange for it to be like that?" she asks Nick, and instantly the template of the movie is set: not real, direct speech, "Did you do that?" or "Was that you?" but genteel speech, with more words than needed, or rather exactly the number of words needed to take a description away from its object, protect characters from emotion, and distance an audience from itself.* Nick nods, and recites the proverb as if it's something he's thought about all his life: "'There is a way which seemeth right to a man, but the end thereof are the ways of death.'"

Within a collapsed story, with plot lines deleted and added as if at random, with characters suddenly pulling their clothes inside out by the need of the film to get from one place to another, with the movie often forgetting it has anything at all to do with the book (who

---

* The obligatory contextualization—every post-silent *Gatsby* movie opens with a 1920s montage—is of a piece. It's purely didactic, a narrative you could call demagogic in its mistrust of the audience, which is to say contempt for it. "Remember the Lindy Hop?" Carey's Nick says to Hussey's Jordan, as if their years together have wiped out her memory. "And before that, the Black Bottom? And before that, the Charleston?" It's a wonder the script didn't insert dates in the dialogue.

knew Tom was a stand-up guy?), and an undercurrent of depression that makes it difficult to remember if in the entire course of the film anyone ever smiles, that's the picture. It's a drama pitched between the poles of Dan Cody—a cackling Henry Hull, as if casting back to his glory role in *The Werewolf of London* in 1935—giving the young Jay Gatsby life lessons and in the end Gatsby realizing it was all a lie and pledging to straighten up and fly right. "What do you want out of life?" Cody asks the boy. "I know how to persevere: work hard and control my instincts," Ladd says—and you think of the character as Ladd, not Gatsby, because he is so barely alive, so suppressed as a body, a face, or a voice that you can't connect him to the thrilling, scary, mysterious person he's supposed to be—and Cody laughs. "Oh, boy," he says—it's the liveliest dialogue in the picture. "You've fallen for the old razzle-dazzle. All that stuff is just to keep the suckers quiet while the wise people rake the chips in. There are special *rules* for smart people. And if a smart man sees something he wants, he just stakes his claim to it. And if somebody is in ahead of him, well, he just moves in anyway. Whatever your dream is, son, you get some money in the bank. Whatever you want, *anything* in the world—you got money, you just take it." And the picture has already shown the fruits of that advice: when Ladd first appears in the film it's as a gangster, with two cars racing on a back road, Ladd in a car driven by Jack Lambert, a film noir heavy who doesn't look quite human, like someone whose features never fully developed, and Ladd shooting the other driver and his gunman dead. So, as Macdonald Carey's Nick says in a voice-over, "Out of the twenties and all they were came Jay . . . Gatsby"—the pause functioning like scare quotes, emphasizing that he's a dubious character, that there is no real Jay Gatsby—"who built a dark empire for himself, because he carried a dream in his heart." At the end, when the empire has failed and the dream is dead, and it's time to live up to the proverb that Nick is just waiting to chisel on his tombstone, Gatsby repents. "Nick, I made a mistake somewhere. I thought I was right, I thought old Dan Cody was right. But look at what I've done to myself and everyone else to get where I am, and for *what*?"—and for the only time in the movie there's a hardness in Ladd's speech, true fury—"To be like the Buchanans?" "Cody said if you don't take what you want you're a sucker," he says, going back to sleep-walking, "but I was the sucker, for believing him." So he's going to take the rap, turn himself in, call the police himself if he has to, and it's as embarrassing to type these lines as it should have been to say them: "I owe that to a kid named Jimmy Gatz—me, Nick"—and he points his thumb to his chest—"*me*. What's going to happen to kids like Jimmy Gatz if guys like me don't tell 'em we're wrong?" He finds redemption just in time to die (in a well-staged scene: at the edge of Gatsby's swimming pool, Wilson shoots Gatsby in the back; not really knowing where he is, he swims to the other side of the pool, where Wilson is waiting, and as he starts to climb out Wilson shoots him point-blank twice), and Nick and Jordan go back to Minneapolis to live without saying much to each other ever after.

When the movie came around again in 1974 you could have made the excuse that because it was a quarter-century since the 1949 version of the twenties, the twenties as the time is put on the screen now will inevitably seem even more unreal—as if there had not been from the beginning of cinema movies that took the past as real, or as if the legend of the twenties had ever gone away. Here all the songs sound corny and the sound is always tinny. Old records play, and you wonder: were they issued with scratches? The songs lie on the screen, inert. They're not music, they're an effect, presented as symbols of the bygone, not as anything anyone ever actually liked: what form do you suppose a life would take that was determined at a decisive moment by the street song nobody cared about? Every woman is by definition a fashion victim; no female character dresses as herself. The dancing seems like a hysterical obligation. Jumping, shouting, throwing arms in the air: everyone seems to be working: you know you're watching a movie with a lot of underpaid people in it. Every gesture might have a pulley at the other end. The Gatsby mansion is stolid and dull, a British pile. Mia Farrow's Daisy seems to be on barbiturates. Robert Redford acts like he's not completely thawed out.

There's one relaxed scene. "They say you killed a man," Sam Waterston's Nick asks Redford's Gatsby. "Just one?" he says. For once his smile is good; he's back in his old Sundance Kid clothes. But you know that's who he'd rather be playing and who you'd rather be watching. It's as if, as Richard Russo hints with his portraits of Wendy and Nolan, he's waiting for Paul Newman to come in and take over the Gatsby role; as if Redford could have put the movie across if someone had recognized that he was really Nick.

All through the 1949 movie, Macdonald Carey's Nick is so insufferable—always offended, always judging, so appalled that he's being pulled in to abet anything so squalid as a meeting between a married woman and a man not her husband he might have had rectitude written into his contract—that Jordan has to tell him to stop being such a stuffed shirt to take the edge off. Waterston starts off flat but grows into the role of Nick as if he's reading the book and, like Scott Shepherd some three decades later, wondering what his role actually is—wondering, as Edmund Wilson seems to have known, in 1922, was the true burden of the time, for what drama his setting is the setting. "He too was a Great Gatsby," as Paul Rosenfeld wrote to Fitzgerald in 1925, "who learned vicariously, I imagine." Gatsby died for Nick's cowardice, for his weakness; Nick's fantasies were dormant or fabulisms, but in Waterston's introspective face, in the way he sometimes swings his body out of its natural hesitations, or tries to, you glimpse how Gatsby has made his own fantasies shared, a patrimony for all Americans, and at the end they surface for Nick, just barely. "The reliable, competent Everyman"—not quite. There's more in Waterston's performance, and it makes sense, in a deeper way it's not any kind of surprise, that twenty years after making the movie he began to play Assistant D.A. Jack McCoy on *Law & Order*, a role he pursued for sixteen seasons, letting you see the character he'd played before while bringing forward the character he hadn't: the ruminative demeanor; the sense of right and justice and the invulnerability of the rich; the fatalism; the lingering alcoholism.*

---

* And, as the Jack McCoy character developed over the years, a sense of where a twenty-first-century Nick might have gone. In a 2002 episode of *Law & Order*, the young Assistant D.A. Serena Southerlyn, trying to nail a company that sells personal information taken off anyone's computer, and checking out her boss to figure out how hard it is to find it, reports back that, perfectly in tune with the war between moderation and outrage that defines both Nick and McCoy, "You listen to a lot of Beatles and fusion jazz. And you have what I can only call a very weird obsession with the Clash."

"HE TOO WAS A GREAT GATSBY"

My recollection from high school was always of this hopeless roman-
tic. I didn't quite see the emptiness of Jay Gatsby. He concentrates
on his love of this woman, but does he really love her? When he
finally has her in his arms, is it enough and is she enough?

—*Leonardo DiCaprio, in Stephen Galloway, "Baz Luhrmann's
Despair, Drive and Gamble Behind 'Great Gatsby,'"* Hollywood
Reporter, *April 24, 2013*

When you first see Gatsby's house in Baz Luhrmann's version
of *The Great Gatsby*, from 2013, almost forty years on from the previous attempt to occupy Afghanistan, you realize you've never seen
the house before, not on film and not when you read the book. Fitzgerald didn't put it on the page and the first directors didn't put it
on the screen. They stated it, a great mansion—in the Ladd movie
you're even told the price, $200,000, "a lot of money"—but they
didn't play with it, they didn't imagine it. You realize you've never
imagined it: what kind of place it must have been to hold the vision
of paradise Gatsby filled it with, to beckon the hordes on Saturday nights, to drape Gatsby himself with the aura of the Count of
Monte Cristo, the man with the false name and the unknowable
fortune who by the thousandth page of the Dumas book seems as
if he controls the world (GATSBY BUYING UP OUR CITY? GATSBY
INVESTS IN SKYSCRAPERS GATSBY PAYS FOR EVERYTHING—

PARTIES, GALAS, SCHOOL, LIBRARY   WALL STREET'S KING? run a flurry of headlines Luhrmann puts up just before the party attended by Daisy and Tom Buchanan begins)—and to be, finally, as empty as any house has ever been.

You don't really see the house until far into the movie, after Gatsby and Daisy's reunion in Nick's cottage, when Gatsby takes her across the lawn to show the place off—before that there have been only glimpses of windows and turrets through foliage and shadows and darkness. Suddenly, there it is, and it throws you back. Could there be a house this all-consuming, so big and grand you can't take it in all at once, a Grand Canyon of a house? Compared to this the Buchanans' mansion across Luhrmann's bay is a bank, a monument to well-kept money, a place that looks as if it were made to ensure that romance could never happen there. Gatsby's house is relentlessly built, yet from the angles by which it's shown it's half supernatural, like the castle in Orson Welles's *Chimes at Midnight* with a swimming pool, something beyond the triviality of a rich man's desires and the limits of an architect's eye. It may in fact be nothing more than the Manly Business School in Sydney—called St. Patrick's Seminary when Luhrmann attended it as a boy—but as Luhrmann rebuilds it on screen, as much an idea as a building, it throws off any place or time.

Once Luhrmann gets to his first Gatsby party, he plunges in as if the whole notional extravaganza has been biding its time, waiting for the right impresario to get the party out of the book and into the open air. The immediacy is like a flood. The parties flow into each other. You can feel people actually having fun, the extras moving as if they're thrilled to be there. There are flashing glimpses of pure style: a movie star bending her long body backward as she strides through the crowd. A woman who looks to be naked under a dress made of nothing but the black skeins of a spider's web.

Though Jelly Roll Morton is on the soundtrack with "Monrovia" and Louis Armstrong with "St. Louis Blues," there's no displacement, no anomaly, in people kicking their legs to the loudest, most lavish hip-hop, to Fergie, Q-Tip, and GoonRock pushing out "A Little Party Never Killed Nobody (All We Got)"—*of course* this is what they'd be dancing to. A combo of black musicians, all in cream suits, plays a foxtrot version of Lana Del Rey's "Young and Beautiful." "Please welcome to the stage, the incredible, Gilda Gray!" shouts the hysterically preening MC, his hair flying as he's had it done so it will do just that, and a woman appears in a shimmy dress to jump the crowd. Josephine Baker undulates and sings. In the setting Luhrmann has made, if Beyoncé were to appear in the flesh to sing Amy Winehouse's "Back to Black" instead of merely tracing the song in the background music, she'd be no more part of the scenery than anyone else. "The one, the only, Beyoncé!" the MC would scream through his megaphone, and people would go mad over her Winged Victory costume until they forgot all about her, about Gilda Gray, Josephine Baker, anyone, in the rush of noise, gossip, alcohol, and the pride of being at the center of the universe.

Luhrmann so fully engages with the setting as Fitzgerald laid it out that the past is present, unfolding as you watch. And then, well into the first party that Nick attends, half an hour into the picture, Gatsby at first like his house is seen—an apparition so imbued with possibility that Luhrmann doesn't let you see him all at once. Nick hears a voice: "Your face is familiar. Weren't you in the Third Division during the war?" Nick looks up at hands, the side of a body. Then the camera pulls back to let you gaze as DiCaprio smiles, and every word Fitzgerald wrote, conjuring up a genie of a smile, is there in a moment so expansive, so welcoming and enclosing, you can't bear the feeling that the moment has to end. Part of the magic of the movie is that, after everything has been brought down, the smile is still there, Gatsby in a tuxedo on his dock, turning from his grave to Nick as Nick watches, as he so desperately tries to imagine this happening, the specter before him one last time, Nick reciting "Gatsby believed in the green light," "and his dream must have seemed so close that he could hardly fail to grasp it," "He did not know that it was already behind him," Nick standing on the dock in the rain as Gatsby turns toward him, a look of confidence in his open face, and no rain where he is standing, because he's dead.

As DiCaprio says, there's an emptiness in Gatsby—a hollowness, all caught in Gatsby's incessantly affected, displacingly secondhand habit of calling anyone he meets "old sport." It was what Maxwell Perkins worried about, asking Fitzgerald very gently if it were possible to say what Gatsby *looked* like, and it was what Fitzgerald recognized, in a panic over Perkins's letter that had him ready to write Gatsby out of the book. In moments—"Some time before he introduced himself I'd got a strong impression that he was picking his words with care"—Gatsby is a specter to himself. He has so completely created himself that in a moment of jeopardy he has no reserves to draw on, no legacy, no history, no one outside of himself to honor, and if he is no longer who he used to be, he is not himself either. But he is absolutely alluring to Nick, because Nick can't imagine himself outside of his life as defined by other people—

Jimmy Gatz has thrown his origins overboard, and Nick can begin a story only by talking about the advice his father gave him, and how he might look like a great-uncle—and Gatsby can. But his emptiness cannot be hollowed out; you can't make a void out of a void. "They're a rotten crowd," Nick says to Gatsby of Daisy and Tom and everyone else who ever crossed his grand threshold, says to Gatsby the last time Nick sees him alive—"You're worth the whole damn bunch put together," and as Nick, Tobey Maguire almost makes the words ring true, as they don't at all ring true on the page.

In the frame Luhrmann gives the story, Tobey Maguire reads a voice-over introduction—Luhrmann's introduction—as the picture begins. Nick Carraway is in a sanitarium, where he's committed himself: "Morbidly Alcoholic," "Insomniac," "Anxiety," "Fits of Anger," reads his patient file. "All of us . . ." he says, his words drawn out, "drank too much"—and there's a hard period at the end of *much*. "The more in tune with the times we were, the more we drank. And none of us, contributed, anything new"—in the last sentence each word pulling against the one before and the one after it with a startling, condemning vehemence. At the most it's a contradiction of the whole idea of modernism. At the least it's a testament that none of the people we're about to meet, Jay Gatsby, Daisy Fay Buchanan, Nick Carraway, Tom Buchanan, Jordan Baker, George Wilson, Myrtle Wilson, and none of the artists, financiers, politicians, movie actors, musicians, and poets floating through Gatsby's parties, had anything to do with the true novelties of the twenties, discoveries in art, thought, and politics whose pull we still feel today. If you listen to Maguire's Nick as he scourges himself, there may be no one in the book worth the whole damn bunch put together but Meyer Wolfsheim, who unlike Nick or Gatsby or Daisy or Nick made history, cutting out a piece of the nation's heart that has never grown back. Except that the whole point of any word written about *The Great Gatsby* is that the book, or Gatsby, or Nick's attempt to explain, precisely cut out a piece of the nation's heart that has never grown back—and that, as David Thomson suggests, Gatsby did make history, acting out a legacy Americans have inherited as inescapably as that of any other founding father.

More than for his *Romeo + Juliet* in 1996 or his *Moulin Rouge!* in 2001, Luhrmann was attacked—dismissed—over *The Great Gatsby* for excess, which is like attacking Mark Twain for ruining a serious book like *Adventures of Huckleberry Finn* with slapstick or Etta James for overdoing a harmless Glenn Miller hit like "At Last" with care. Along with the unveiling of Gatsby's house, the realism of his parties, or casting Elizabeth Debicki as Jordan—at six-foot-three the Jordan Playboy walking, a praying mantis in a Louise Brooks haircut, an actress who can produce the illusion of any movement with her eyes—Luhrmann's Wolfsheim is too much, and so much so that strains in the story that in the novel lie dormant now breathe for the first time.

In the book, and as he appears in the Ladd and Redford movies, as at first in *Gatz*, Wolfsheim is a Jewish caricature, his English smeared by Yiddish, and you can picture him as a sad sack little hustler with a ratty face. With Jay-Z's "100$ Bill" swirling through the crowd in the private club where Gatsby has invited Nick, Luhrmann brings him on as the seventy-year-old Bollywood "Star of the Millennium" Amitabh Bachchan, not as tall as Debicki but taller than any other man in the picture, taking up more space in a room, physically commanding in a double-breasted gray suit that throws off a silvery light. Surrounded by his own moustaches, with a white beard under dark sideburns and a broad-brimmed white hat, he's pure glamour, far more alive than Maguire or DiCaprio as they sit at his side. DiCaprio's Gatsby absorbs his energy; Maguire's Nick is afraid of it. And you get a sense of why Fitzgerald might have hung back from the scene even as he imagined it. We meet Wolfsheim in the novel's 1922, a mere three years after Arnold Rothstein pulled off the deal of the century.* It was three years before *The Great Gatsby* appeared in 1925, and six years before Arnold Rothstein was shot to death in a hotel on Seventh Avenue in New York City in 1928. The scene with Wolfsheim wouldn't have had half the conviction that it does, that "He's the man who fixed the World's Series back in 1919" like a bomb under Nick's chair, if Rothstein hadn't, in the novel's fixed moment in time, as those who picked it up in 1925 would have known, gotten away with it. Before Luhrmann put Bachchan in the role, Wolfsheim always seemed too small for what he was supposed to have done. Bachchan, a dandy, expansive, all broad gestures and wary movements, carries the event with him like a cloak; he's getting away with it as you watch. In Luhrmann's version of the confrontation in the Plaza Hotel, when Tom

---

* It's an event that might be at the heart of baseball as legend, and the real foundation not only of the Jazz Age but of the Baseball Hall of Fame—if Shoeless Joe isn't there, the World Series was never fixed. There is a special "Guide to the Black Sox" collection, which may be viewed by appointment only.

Buchanan hammers Gatsby as the mobster's flunky—"How does a reputable banker like Walter Chase find himself up to his eyeballs in debt to a little kike like Wolfsheim?"—you can feel Tom's intimidation, you've already seen that Bachchan's Wolfsheim has three inches on Joel Edgerton's Buchanan, and you can, looking back on Bachchan's appearance in the film, feel that the slur would slide off of him like feathers, just as every word that Tom flings at Gatsby draws blood.

In the novel, the emptiness DiCaprio found in his own character may be elided by the crime-novel finale and the gorgeous, allusive writing. Fitzgerald said as much to Edmund Wilson when the book came out: "The worst fault in it, I think is a BIG FAULT: I gave no account (and had no feeling about or knowledge of) the emotional relations between Gatsby and Daisy from the time of their reunion to the catastrophe"—a gap Luhrmann fills, showing DiCaprio and Carey Mulligan's Daisy rolling in bed in the weeks after they meet again—"However, the lack is so astutely concealed by the retrospect of Gatsby's past and by blankets of excellent prose that no one has noticed it—tho everyone has felt the lack and called it by another name. Mencken said (in a most enthusiastic letter received today) that the only fault was that the central story was trivial and a sort of anecdote (that is because he has forgotten his admiration for Conrad and adjusted himself to the sprawling novel) and I felt that what he really missed was the lack of any emotional backbone at the very height of it." But he was angry, maybe at himself, certainly at Mencken too: "Without making any invidious comparisons between Class A and Class C, if my novel is an anecdote then so is *The Brothers Karamazov.* From one angle the latter could be reduced into a detective story."

That sense of the rug being slowly pulled out from under Gatsby's feet gives the novel its detective-story suspense, and it is also what leaves the character invisible and unknowable even to himself—that's the cheap betrayal of Alan Ladd's "I owe that to a kid named Jimmy Gatz—me," the simple notion that you can just run the movie backward and begin again from the beginning.

In the story *The Great Gatsby* has been telling since its characters began to speak, this is where Luhrmann's movie comes in. An Australian who'd bought up rights to a shelf of novels with no clear idea of what if anything he'd do with them saw that the real drama, the ordinary drama, the love story, was not between Gatsby and Daisy but between Gatsby and Nick. Luhrmann saw that just as Nick had to be given a greater intellectual presence, so that the introspection playing on Sam Waterston's face would play into Nick's mind and come out of Tobey Maguire's mouth in words, even visions, Gatsby had to be given a physical presence he never had before—not in the novel, not in the allusions to him piling up in every form of discourse over the decades, not on the stage, and not on the screen. He has to look exactly like himself, a self no one could picture before but once glimpsed in the flesh would be recognized instantly and absolutely. He must have the beauty to make his case: to make you feel, in the end, that something at once small and immeasurable has been lost. DiCaprio could do that, as Ladd and Redford couldn't—as it seems they didn't understand that that was their role, that was the hollow mountain, the mountain that would cave in with one false move, that they had to climb. And here, in the way that in their own minds and in the minds of people watching, actors carry their roles with them, certain roles that Di-Caprio played before he played Gatsby play into the drama, and increase the pressure of the performance as he understands it and we receive it: his penniless twenty-year-old midwesterner Jack Dawson in *Titanic* in 1997, all broad gestures and unbreakable nerve; his rough, Southie Boston cop Billy Costigan passing as a mobster in *The Departed* in 2006, fear of exposure tightening around his shoulders in almost every scene, then so shockingly ambushed, dead in the blink of an eye. They too are there in every footstep, and the movie creates and vivifies a character Fitzgerald could not.

DiCaprio has the glow Fitzgerald wrote around his character. In certain moments he seems tremendously young, no more than nineteen; at others he is so handsome he seems like the realization of humanity. At times the contradictions of his character's identity almost break the surface of DiCaprio's portrayal, or they do break the surface, and when that happens it's an appalling thing to see — to see Gatsby losing hold of his character, a man losing hold of his invented self, which has become the only real self he has, a self so complete he could look in a mirror and not recognize himself. Di-Caprio can convey mastery and terror in almost the same instant, as in the crux of the movie when, at the club where Wolfsheim has appeared, in a scene that prepares the ground for its match at the end of the story, Gatsby's mask splits for the first time as Tom Buchanan calls out of the speakeasy hubbub to Nick and then strolls into the frame.

DiCaprio freezes. Anger, fear, most of all bitterness — over the whole vicious lottery of birth — pass across his face. He looks violently alone, his sense of isolation so strong it's like a force field silencing the noise of the room even as it goes on. Nick introduces Gatsby to Tom, who shrugs him off as if he's a bug: "Yeah," Joel Edgerton says, not even looking at him, whoever he is. The expression on DiCaprio's face is so awful you can't look at it, a boy who's been humiliated by his own father in front of everyone and who now has to watch as his dad looks down on him, grinning: *Thought you could get away with it, didn't you, little man?* DiCaprio doubles down on his sense of his character: he empties Gatsby's face so completely you glimpse his future destruction. And DiCaprio plays against the scene, with rich gestures, in his beautiful clothes and beautiful cars trying to negate it, but always carrying the scene inside his performance, the rest of the way.

"I know you like to watch," Joel Edgerton's Tom, his terrifyingly convincing bully of privilege, says to Tobey Maguire as his Nick tries to get away from Tom and Myrtle's party in New York like the guy in Randy Newman's "Mama Told Me Not to Come." "I remember that from college." And so a perverse sexual charge is injected into Maguire's not-yet-developed role as the witness, as the "And I only am escaped alone to tell thee." "Now," says the Yale football hero Buchanan, gesturing at the women who've crashed into the apartment, at Myrtle's devil-in-a-green-dress sister Catherine, who when waterboy Nick turns down her offer of a "nerve pill" puts it in her mouth and kisses it into his, "do you want to sit on the sidelines and *watch*—or do you want to play ball?" He plays ball. "I have been drunk just twice in my life," says Fitzgerald's Nick, in this scene—it's always read like a typo. "I had been drunk just twice in my life," says Luhrmann's Nick, just before getting sweatingly, swimmingly drunk, and it's as if Luhrmann and Maguire are telling a story that Fitzgerald and Nick lied about.

Maguire is now back in the sanitarium, performing the writing therapy his doctor has prescribed, trying to set down the story of the summer that ended with him walking through the streets of New York in a drunken haze, five days' growth on his face, his tie loose, still taking the train from Long Island to Manhattan every day and walking to work but never entering his building, walking from one end of Broadway to the other in clothes that are fraying and spotted, that in two weeks will rot on him the way a junkie can begin to rot when he or she is still alive.

At the party, people are stripping. Nick is in his undershirt. On the fire escape of a building across the street, there's a black trumpet player—Nick hears him, and then all sound falls away as he looks out the window. In the other building, all sorts of tiny, ordinary dramas are taking place: a family sitting down to dinner, a black woman resting her arms on her windowsill. With rough, unpretty features, she's so beautiful the eye of the film stops blinking, because her face stays in front of your eyes as the frames of the film click on. She's engaged in the most common act, doing something everyone has done, maybe at peace, maybe not, thinking through her life, asking herself if it's worth it. The scene is more like a painting than a scene, joining, as the film critic Mick LaSalle answered when asked if there were images in movies that returned to him without bidding, the likes of "the people who just happened to be on the platform when the Lumière brothers filmed a train coming into a station in 1895—and now they're on film forever. These few seconds will turn out to be the most lasting thing they ever did with their lives." With this shot of an imagined woman placing a strange and undeniable element of realism into this imaginary tableau, that's the feeling at this moment, as Nick watches a woman who isn't watching him. You know that even though he's too drunk to remember a thing from this night, once a year, once every ten years, that face will reappear in his memory, which will never tell him where and when he saw her, or why she owns some repeating seconds of his life.

"I know you like to watch" — he sees a "casual watcher in the street," Luhrmann's Nick says, as in his undershirt he looks from the window at himself standing at a lamppost below, well dressed in tie, jacket, and hat, "and I was him, too," his voice says, as Maguire sits writing in the sanitarium. "Looking up and wondering. I was within, and without." The last lines aren't necessary: what's shown is so strong it doesn't need to be told. But as soon as that false note is sounded it's swept away. With the party going on behind him, Nick again looks out the window, at another apartment house, and in different postures, standing, sitting, on a bed, in every window the same young black woman and the same old, fat, bald white man play out the same story, like a board game in a nightmare. It might be the woman Nick saw before. The man might be him, thirty years from this night, when he's forgotten her, just as he'll forget this woman he's paying for love.

"He too was a Great Gatsby": this is Luhrmann drawing Nick out, giving him the life that, when it begins to slip away from him, will be worth keeping, or anyway writing down. The narrator, Gilbert Seldes wrote in his *Dial* review of *The Great Gatsby*, was "obviously intended to be much more significant than he is.

The author's appetite for life is so violent that he found the personality of the narrator an obstacle, and simply ignored it once actual people were in motion." When Luhrmann first sets Maguire's voice over the screen, at the opening of the movie, it's Nick's own blocked appetite for life that begins to emerge, and his voice is not an obstacle but a secret passageway.

There is a twenties lament on a clarinet, sounding very distant, and the flickering black-and-white deco design of a metal gate with *JG* emblazoned at its center, just above the initials in the open space of the design, a glowing, rounded light. It's corny—it's the opening of *Citizen Kane*—but it's a movie, and it moves you on: the now receding gate becomes a globe of illumination. The camera retreats from it farther, until it's a pinprick of green light, flicking on and off. Behind an image of Manhasset Bay, the view across to the green light at the end of a dock, there's somber movie music, but the image itself, suspended, is like a song, again corny, but you're listening. You hear Maguire's Nick, his voice hovering over this image, beginning very tentatively, gravelly and flat. His father, as in the beginning of the novel, is giving him instruction, but not quite the instruction Fitzgerald gave his Nick. "In my younger and more vulnerable years," Maguire says, "my father gave me some advice"—and the image is shifting to winter—"'Try to see the *best* in people.' As a consequence, I'm inclined to reserve all judgments. But even I, have a *limit*."

You see a vast institutional building covered in snow, with ice in the water before it. And so the story, still on the image of the bay and the light, begins with drapes of portent and dread, like a western already building up to the final shootout. But here, at the beginning, something more interesting has happened. That flat and gravelly scrape in Nick's voice has turned into the hard-boiled tone taken up by the detectives who would come after this one: Hammett's Continental Op, Chandler's Philip Marlowe, Macdonald's Lew Archer, Walter Mosley's Easy Rawlins.* Here at the start, Nick's voice has been established not only as one of authority, but as that of the final arbiter of the story. And in the moment, whatever that story will turn out to be seems less compelling than the voice itself.

Like DiCaprio's Gatsby, Tobey Maguire's Nick takes in characters that sketched out the role that Maguire is constructing now — characters that, playing on the actor's clear memory of the other eyes looking through those of the Maguire who is now Nick Carraway, are as much a part of his authority as anything else. In *The Ice Storm* in 1994 there is his sixteen-year-old prep school student Paul Hood coming home to his parents' spouse-swapping Darien, Connecticut, for Thanksgiving, narrating in voice-over about the Fantastic Four comic book he's reading. As with his teenage TV fan David in 1998 in *Pleasantville*, transported by means of a magic remote proffered by Don Knotts's demonic repairman into the black-and-white fifties *Father Knows Best*–perfect family show he and his sister watch as if it's both a joke and, compared with their own broken family, utopia, or as the young writer James Leer living with a

---

* "How can you possibly know so much about the details of other people's lives?" a woman asks Lew Archer. "Other people's lives are my business," he says. "And your passion?" "And my passion. And my obsession, too, I guess. I've never been able to see much in the world besides the people in it." *The Far Side of the Dollar* (1965).

dissolving family in *Wonder Boys* in 2000, and even as Peter Parker in the *Spider-Man* pictures, each of his characters is always watching, thinking, wondering what's going on around him and why, bright with enthusiasm when he sees or mentally glimpses something new, something he wasn't prepared for. He could be the same character in each, an impression that comes out of the closed circle of 1990s movies about middle-class white people—Joan Allen, looking as if she hasn't eaten in years, plays his mother in both *The Ice Storm* and *Pleasantville*, just as Katie Holmes plays his friend and someone else's girlfriend in *The Ice Storm* and *Wonder Boys*.

In *The Cider House Rules*, from 1999, set mostly during the early forties in Maine, where Maguire's Homer Wells has grown up in an orphanage run by nuns, under the wing of Michael Caine's obstetrician and, everyone knows, abortionist, the eyes see the farthest. They're always curious, but what was enthusiasm before is now wonder, awe, registering his shock over human depravity. A toughness in his character, a quiet determination, emerges as the movie goes on—as, without any formal education, with Caine's tutelage he too goes into "the doctor business," a phrase he pulls off as if it describes both his skill and his illegitimacy. He's been trained as a physician to understand that anything can happen, that anyone can cause anything, by accident or by design, and as that knowledge accumulates his eyes shift into a hard stare: accusatory, vengeful, but he isn't going to say what it's meant to say. That's for the person on the other end to figure out.

This is the look his Nick will need as he watches the tragedy of the story take its shape—not Gatsby's murder, which he doesn't witness, because Gatsby was already dead. Buchanan killed him in the room at the Plaza, and that Nick saw, in every detail, and Tobey Maguire's Nick has to see more than Fitzgerald's. "After Gatsby's death the East was haunted for me," Fitzgerald's Nick says, but Maguire has to take the haunt into himself.

Lana Del Rey's "Young and Beautiful" has already played its way through the movie. There's just a floating sensation as Daisy sees Gatsby's house for the first time—it's all in the sweep of the melody, so expansive that it can carry the singer's slightly acrid, morbid tone so comfortably that her voice can seem to float on itself. "Will you still love me, when I'm no longer, young and beautiful?"—you don't quite notice when the song fades away. The song will come back, barely audible as it passes over the bay like weather, the question distant but still insistent, as if it's this place, as seen by Dutch sailors' eyes, that's no longer young and beautiful. The song will come back as Gatsby and Daisy break away from the party where she's come with Tom, and they kiss against a tree—Lana Del Rey has the voice that Daisy doesn't, not Fitzgerald's Daisy, not Carey Mulligan's. About the same age—Lana Del Rey was twenty-eight in 2013, Daisy a year or two older in 1922—Lana Del Rey's voice plays as Daisy's second mind, saying what Daisy would say if she could, in the way that she'd say it, but she doesn't have the words, doesn't have the confidence Lana Del Rey has. It's the confidence, the voice says, of the already dead, which Mulligan's Daisy may be, but no one will ever tell her, and as the song hangs over her she's a character in a movie, it's on the soundtrack, and her character doesn't hear it.

The drama—the drama of open, then closing possibilities—has already ended when Edgerton's Tom, shifting back and forth between mere anger and menace, has charged the Plaza room with an unbearable, skin-crawling tension, where every move seems fatal, where it seems that not one false move but any true move, or any move at all, will bring everything to ruin. "I never loved him," Mulligan says, but as the words hang in the air a question mark drifts onto the last word, and Buchanan sees his opening. He does know her better than Gatsby does—and he breaks her. And you both see and hear all this, hear as you listen in a movie but also as you listen to characters speak as you read, in Luhrmann's hotel room, with Luhrmann now pushing on past the book as Fitzgerald wrote it, letting Gatsby and Tom say what they have never said before, what they've always wanted to say, all of it coming out now with the force of having been suppressed for so long—it's shown, in all of its manipulative brutality, as it's never been shown before.

"I need to speak to Daisy alone," Gatsby says, and Edgerton offers a big, expansive, be-my-guest wave. He's already won, and in the pleasure of winning he keeps hitting: "Daisy, can't you see who this guy is? He's a front for Wolfsheim, the *gangster*, to get his claws into a respectable man like Walter Chase." With his smile still somehow real, DiCaprio's Gatsby is ready for that—but he doesn't understand the game. He doesn't understand that it was fixed before any of them were born. "The only thing respectable about you, old sport," Luhrmann's Gatsby says to Tom, now in the new territory of the story that Luhrmann has staked out, "is your money. Your money, that's it. Now I've just as much as you. That means we're equal"—and however that might have sounded in 1925, if it had been in Fitzgerald's pages, to hear it in the twenty-first century is to hear screaming alarms going off all over the city. *No, no, don't say that, don't you see what a bomb you've handed him, that he's going to throw right back in your face?* In an America where many people have enough money to personally fund every election in the United States in a single election year, for every office on every level, local, state, and national, for every school board, city council, mayoralty, state legislature, governorship, U.S. representative, U.S. senator, president, and not, in terms of their own private well-being, even notice the expenditure, as soon as Gatsby speaks you know that his money isn't real, and Buchanan's is not only real but untouchable. "We're equal"—DiCaprio smiles again as he says it, but now it's not a good smile. He seems like he's spinning a line, as if he doesn't believe what he's saying but is betting somebody might.

In a speech that matches his rant about *The Rise of the Colored Empires*—when in the film Edgerton goes off at the table about how the white race will be wiped out, he tweaks the face of a black servant standing attendance—Luhrmann's Buchanan pushes it all farther. "We're all white here," Jordan has said after Tom started off the final, fated afternoon with his "next they'll throw everything overboard and have intermarriage between black and white," but now the feeling that Gatsby may not, in a deeper sense of the idea, or just below the skin, be white at all, deserving of the rights those endowed by their creator with whiteness are guaranteed, is hovering in the air. "Oh no, *noooooooo*," Edgerton says with deadly amusement. "We're different. I am"—he gestures at Nick and Jordan—"they are. She is. We're all different from you." His cadence stops just short of sing-song, but it has the cool rhythmic momentum of unquestionable power—this is the voice that's full of money. "You see," Buchanan says, explaining to an inferior who has somehow wandered into the wrong place, "we were born different. It's in our blood. And nothing that you do, or say—or steal, or dream up, will ever change that." Again, *in the blood*, that first racist spew that started off the summer now paying off at the end of it—that DiCaprio's face then comes apart in rage, as he rushes at Tom and holds his fist over his face, is no matter. Gatsby's face is red and covered in sweat. Buchanan's face is calm, and worse than that— relaxed, a look on his face that says, *Really, old sport?* Edgerton rises, and with sadistic deliberation puts his forehead against Di-Caprio's, and pushes it back. What happens under the red white and blue? The pursuit of happiness, if you have the nerve, even the nerve to make yourself up—the pursuit of happiness, and if you don't have the nerve, the wages are shame. But here the wages are the same. *I had the courage!* Gatsby shouts at Buchanan, maybe at everyone else in the room, too, maybe at the rich room itself— first with hysterical shouts of "*YOU SHUT UP! SHUT UP! SHUT UUUUUUPPPPPP!*" and then mutely, DiCaprio's disheveled face making the noise. Under the red white and blue, flying in front of the Plaza with the flags of whatever foreign dignitaries might have been in residence that day, Tom has read him out of America, out of the America where "all men are created equal," where "they are endowed by their Creator with certain unalienable Rights, that among these are Life, Liberty and the pursuit of Happiness," and into the America where, as Walter Mosley says, to have faith is to be a fool.

With that murder, with that soul killing, in the final shots of the film, the dead Gatsby on his dock, reaching out across the bay, turning back to Nick and smiling past the rain, as in the sanitarium Nick types out his last words, as they appear on the screen, "And one fine morning — So we beat on, boats against the current," their sentimentality finally rings true, because now, in this movie, as not before, the tragedy is complete, because you have seen everything that was lost. Nick has finally been placed at the center of the story, where he has become both the grounding and the test of all of its characters, which as archetypes and metaphors and even catchphrases will travel through the century and into the next. He is finally the hero of the story because, unlike anyone else, he has thought about it — he will always be thinking about it. There's no catharsis, no relief. There's not even a sense of transport, or a moment when the movement toward the last words pauses, and asks you to imagine yourself into the eyes of Dutch sailors and the fresh, green breast of the new world as it appears before them, because here Nick doesn't write that paragraph, he doesn't recite it, and you are deprived of its beauty, of the way the paragraph is beyond any story, any moral, any punishment, as the stars at the end of Philip Roth's *I Married a Communist* are beyond sin, betrayal, lies, and death. ". . . borne back ceaselessly into the past" — as Nick types the words there's only an unanswerable apprehension of defeat — of humiliation, cynicism, ruin, waste, pointlessness — that enveloping vast carelessness — and a sighting ahead, to see Nick, having finished his writing cure, leaving the sanitarium, making his way into the future, most likely marked by the story he's told, hobbled by it into silence, never writing another word.

FABLE

On the wall beside every table there was a box with which one could operate the jukebox without getting up. I put in a quarter and selected Otis Redding's "Sitting on the Dock of the Bay." I thought of the great Gatsby and became more self-assured than ever before in my life: to the point that I lost all awareness of myself. I would do many things differently. I would become unrecognizable! I ordered a hamburger and a Coca-Cola.

—*Peter Handke*, Short Letter, Long Farewell, 1972

I went inside the club, where the late afternoon crowd were enjoying themselves, if gamblers can be said to enjoy themselves. . . . They pulled convulsively at the handles of one-armed bandits, as if the machines were computers that would answer all their questions. Am I getting old? Have I failed? Am I immature? Does she love me? Why does he hate me? Hit me, jackpot, flood me with life and liberty and happiness.

—*Ross Macdonald*, The Zebra-Striped Hearse, 1962

The Great Gatsby can be read as a fable of the Crash—a writer's instinct, his feeling out the boundaries of history as it was being made, or ignored, that not only was the great dance around the Golden Calf sure to lead to ruin, it should. Jay-Z heard it that way on Baz Luhrmann's *Gatsby* soundtrack on his "100$ Bill," playing through the dance of Gatsby, Nick, Tom, and Meyer Wolfsheim in the New York speak: "Go numb until I can't feel, or might pop this pill / Stock markets just crash, now I'm just a bill." Even the dollar loses its voice. In historiographical time—the kind of time art and history make when you realize that artists sometimes write more complete history than scholars—you can hear the replacement of Gatsby's parties by Skip James's "Hard Time Killing Floor Blues." "Isolated during the European War, we had begun combing the unknown South and West for folkways and pastimes, and there were more ready to hand," Fitzgerald wrote in 1931; that same year, the acerbic minor-key Mississippi blues guitarist traveled to Grafton, Wisconsin, to record for the Paramount label. The recording director asked James if he had anything about the Depression—a topical song might sell. Playing off of Stephen Foster's "Hard Times," what James came up with, like that, had no time or place fixed in it. "Sometimes I'd be laying down through the night and there are things that come to me, and I'll get up and jot it down," James said in 1964. "Maybe just the *title* of a song. Skip, you could make a song out of just about anything, the cigarette blues, the paperback blues, Co-cola bottle, most anything. And then I get up and jot that down. Perhaps maybe, the next morning, I see this title—the next day I see this title, I supposed to compose a song. And in my later time, it look like things have come to me, I don't know why. . . . I don't know, I just can't fathom that out, but yet and still things come to me. And I can get up through the night and start playing something I never heard." James took the long view: a song that sounded right the day it reached the public had to speak to publics born after the singer was dead. He opened "Hard Time Killing Floor Blues," with soft, fatalistic notes on his guitar, descending, the slow, grudging rhythm of someone dragging himself down the street, taking the listener down, shutting out the lights, with the last word of a sentence un-spoken, a chord left hanging in the air. With a high, religious moan, James seemed to be dragging the future behind himself. It was as if the whole country could fit into two lines: "People are drifting from door to door / Can't find no heaven, I don't care where they go," which meant there was no place the people in the song could go that would take them in—and, behind that, that the singer didn't care. The song is hard, unkind, unforgiving, until the end, when the singer might be laughing after picking up a copy of *The Great Gatsby* someone had dropped in the street: "You know, you'll say you had money / You better be sure."

The market for blues had exploded in the 1920s. From Chi-cago to New Orleans, from Harlem to Houston, Bessie Smith, Blind Lemon Jefferson, and Charley Patton could sell tens, even hundreds of thousands of copies of a single disc, but the Crash dropped the bottom out of the market. A record might cost seventy-five cents, but seventy-five cents could feed a family, if you had it. James's records—"Devil Got My Woman" on one side, with "Cy-press Grove Blues" on the other, "Hard Time Killing Floor Blues" with "Cherry Ball Blues," "If You Haven't Any Hay Get on Down the Road" with "22–20 Blues," and a few more—were and remain singular works of American art, but they didn't sell. In the late 1940s and early 50s, right about the time when people again began to talk about *The Great Gatsby*, when collectors began to comb the South for James's records, they found, then and in the decades to come, almost nothing: six copies of "Devil Got My Woman," five of "Hard Time Killing Floor Blues," for most of the rest two copies, and for one, only one. I've always treasured the fantasy that this was no accident: that having put aside his guitar after the failure of his music, James set out to destroy as many copies of his records as he could, purposely leaving only a handful in the world—not to make them more valuable on some market to come, but so, if and when they were ever found, they would glow with the power of fable. *What were they?* People would ask. *Who was he? Where did this come from?*

What if the same were true of *The Great Gatsby*, with the book and James's songs touching hands across the years before and after the Crash that anyone can now see enacted in Gatsby's life, passed into the devastation enacted on tens of millions, a World Series fixed for real, all the people left with nothing for the bets they never placed? Not only that it would take a generation before people began to hear the tunes behind Fitzgerald's words, but what if, by the time people began to look for the records Skip James had made, there were only three copies of *The Great Gatsby* left in the world?

It's not until about 1948 that the country begins to breathe again, when after nearly twenty years of depression and war, there is a kind of mass psychic awakening—*My God! We're not dead!*— that would send an anarchic spirit into the air. It was just before the country was ready to turn to Fitzgerald's short book as a story that, as Harold Bloom said with such warmth of the likes of "The Weight" and "Across the Great Divide," was, as an account of the American predicament, always there.

That may be right. It's also wrong. The book may serve as a social document. But as Jay-Z goes on in "100$ Bill," repeating an old commonplace, "History don't repeat itself it rhymes." The book seeks affinities. It seeks its own readers, who read the book back to itself, and the book changes, and moves through time, rewriting the history not only of 1922, or 1925, but of all the time that it has crossed over. People aspire to so acute a fable about a national life. But what makes people think that it is a social document, a social critique, is the music of the writing—and while anyone can aspire to the social document and realize that aspiration, not very many people can come close to the siren song that called them to it, which is why Philip Roth, from "Goodbye, Columbus" in 1959 to *The Human Stain* more than forty years later, kept after it so long. It was why, as Ross Macdonald admitted in 1972, from at least *The Galton Case* in 1959 through *The Zebra-Striped Hearse, The Far Side of the Dollar* in 1965, *Black Money* in 1966, and *The Instant Enemy* in 1968, he was rewriting *The Great Gatsby* over and over again, and how, from the start, with *The Moving Target* in 1949, he was trying to lead Lew Archer into a life Nick Carraway should have lived. And it is why Raymond Chandler, finally giving up on the idea of writing the movie, the real movie, in 1953 began his book *The Long Goodbye*, even dropping the West Egg mansion into Los Angeles ("Whoever built that place was trying to drag the Atlantic seaboard over the Rockies. He was trying hard, but he hadn't made it"), with his Daisy killing not only his Myrtle but her own husband (an alcoholic best-selling novelist drowning in self-loathing because every word he writes dishonors his hero, F. Scott Fitzgerald), with his Gatsby, Terry Lennox ("He had been a man it was impossible to dislike," Marlowe says of the guy who insists on calling him "old top." "How many do you meet in a lifetime that you can say that about?"), taking the rap but then with the help of his mob pals from the war faking his own death, only to return to Los Angeles, disguised as a courier, to his Nick, Philip Marlowe, the one-time Lennox now a perfumed Señor Cisco Maioranos, so repulsive in his perfect manners that even after he drops the act he all but oozes embalming fluid. The small tragedy that wafts into the room is that Chandler's Lennox and Marlowe, his Gatsby and Nick, have nothing to say to each other. "He turned and walked across the floor and out. I watched the door close. I listened to his steps going away down the imitation marble corridor. After a while they got faint, then they got silent. I kept on listening anyway. What for? Did I want him to stop suddenly and turn and come back and talk me out of the way I felt? Well, he didn't. That was the last I saw of him."

As with the words Skip James does and doesn't sing, the music in *The Great Gatsby* is in the play of echoes Fitzgerald sets in motion throughout the book, until, at the end, they fold together, and the sound they make is that of a distant gong. Then you can hear that Gatsby's vision of paradise is to be realized not in his life, but in the passage of the Dutch sailors, when they made landfall on the fresh, green breast of the New World in 1609. And if you hear that, you also hear the sound of the gong growing louder, as the tragedy of the twinned images expands to take in the whole of the country, as desire and fact, illusion and reality, truth and lie.

Truth and lie: in July 2019, in New York, five hundred people came together for the National Conservatism Conference, "organized," Jennifer Schuessler reported in the *New York Times*, "by the Edmund Burke Foundation, a newly formed public affairs institute." A highlight was a talk by Rich Lowry, the editor of the *National Review*, called "Why America Is Not an Idea," which set about to dismantle what Lowry named "one of our most honored clichés": the notion that what America is is nothing more than the promise the country made to itself at its founding, the promise of life, liberty, and the pursuit of happiness, which after 1776 was set loose in the land as a train that would never come to rest. No, Lowry said, it was culture: a very particular culture, made by particular Americans. He was followed, Schuessler wrote, by the University of Pennsylvania law professor Amy Wax, who pursued the same argument with a harder edge. "She dismissed the idea," Schuessler said, "that immigrants somehow became American simply by living here, which Ms. Wax (borrowing a term used by white nationalists and self-described 'race realists') mocked as the 'magic dirt' argument. There's no reason that 'people who come here will quickly come to think, live and act just like us,' she said. Immigration policy, she said, should take into account 'cultural compatibility.'" Wax was not talking about all of the cultures that make American culture; the music of Skip James, as the product of a black man, was not American culture. You could hear the echo hammering back out of Baz Luhrmann's movie as his Tom read his Gatsby out of the country, erasing him from its history: "We were born different. It's in our blood. There's nothing you can do, say, steal, or dream up—"

This is what was already behind Fitzgerald, and behind the reader as she or he is sucked into Fitzgerald's last page, as Scott Shepherd makes his way through it like a navigator, and Luhrmann lets Tobey Maguire leave it hanging in the air: the discovery, the taking possession of the place where Gatsby would come to life, centuries before he was born, when the green light was lit. When all of this comes together—one life playing out the blighted, stubborn idea of America, then you have tragedy slamming you and the country down to the ground. Then any citizen is made to put on Nick Carraway's clothes, walk in his shoes, and watch, as Gatsby's private catastrophe moves on, dropping the shadow of the red white and blue, now a banner, now a shroud, over the country, the land and the idea.

ACKNOWLEDGMENTS

My first thanks go to Steve Wasserman, who I first met in 1971, and with whom I've had a writer-editor relationship since 1979, when as an op-ed editor at the *Los Angeles Times* he assigned me a premature obituary for John Wayne. He got me started on what began as a very different book than the one I wrote, but I never would have stumbled on what it became without him. Emmerich Anklam, his assistant and coeditor at Heyday Books in Berkeley, gave invaluable advice on finding a real book inside a misconception. John Donatich of Yale University Press, through three books now, has been an invaluable source of support, sober encouragement and judgment, and most of all trust. At Yale I have also relied on Danielle D'Orlando, Abigail Storch, Dorothea Halliday, Erica Hanson, Maureen Noonan, page designer Nancy Ovedovitz, and publicist Jennifer Doerr. When Sonia Shannon's jacket design arrived, yes was the only word to say: it was first-draft perfect. Once again I have had the privilege and pleasure of working with designated-but-so-much-more-than copy editor Dan Heaton. At the Brandt & Hochman Literary Agents I had the calming and imaginative counsel of Emily Forland, and of her colleagues Emma Patterson, Marianne Merola, Henry Thayer, and Gabe Szabo.

Jill Vuchetich of the Walker Art Center in Minneapolis generously opened her archives to allow me to watch the video of the original American performance of *Gatz* whenever I wanted. Cecily Marcus saw that performance and made sure I didn't consider missing it when I had the chance to see it years later. *The Great Gatsby* was not required reading at Menlo-Atherton High in the early sixties—we read *Ivanhoe, A Tale of Two Cities,* and *Giants in the Earth*—but it was at St. Paul Central High, where then Jenny Bernstein first read it, and I first read her copy.

Some of the pages here draw on work that has appeared before: parts of "A Patriotic Swerve" on an essay on patriotism for the *Village Voice* in 1976 and on a commencement address for the American Studies Program at the University of California at Berkeley in 2006, while much of "A Book Everyone Has Heard Of" is adapted from an essay in *A New Literary History of America,* published by Harvard in 2009. Kathleen Moran at Berkeley and Werner Sollors at Harvard, good friends and generous scholars, are colleagues anyone would be lucky to have.

Thanks go too to Emily Marcus, to Steve Perry, fellow Lana Del Rey fan, who took the dedication photo, to Daniel Marcus, David Ross and David J. Rhodes of the School of Visual Arts in New York, Scott Woods, Michael Lesy, David Thomson, Alice Kaplan, Nathalie Batraville, Pat Schaffer, Lindsay Waters, Anne Margaret Daniel, Paula Bernstein, William Bernstein, John Collins of Elevator Repair Service, and especially Jim Miller—for this book, and others before it.

INDEX

Books are noted with credit to author, recordings to recording artist, and films to director or leading actor or both—whoever has made their way into common memory as the principal figure. Other productions identified as seems most useful.